The Resiliency Workbook

Bounce Back Stronger, Smarter
& With Real Self-Esteem

Nan Henderson, M.S.W.

Resiliency In Action, Inc.
Solvang, CA

For information about permission to reproduce selections from this book, write to
Permissions, Resiliency In Action, P.O. Box 1242, Solvang, CA 93464

For information about discounts for bulk purchases, please contact
Resiliency In Action, nhenderson@resiliency.com
or call 800-440-5171

Cover and book design by Paula Pugh
Index by Michael E. Bell
Manufacturing by Gorham Printing

Library of Congress Cataloging-in-Publication Data
Henderson, Nan.
The Resiliency Workbook: Bounce Back Stronger, Smarter & With Real Self-Esteem / Nan Henderson.
Includes index.
ISBN 978-0-393-70743-4

Control Number: 2012912391

Resiliency In Action, Inc. P.O. Box 1242, Solvang, CA 93464
www.resiliency.com

For Bruce,
the most wonderful mirror of my life,
with love & gratitude

Acknowledgements

This book is the direct result of invaluable interactions I have had with the thousands of people who have attended my resiliency presentations over the past twenty years. I am very grateful for the insight, wisdom, and inspiration that resulted from these interactions.

In addition, I so appreciate the resiliency researchers and inspirational writers I quote in this book. The resiliency perspective is now at least part of almost every field of human endeavor due to your pioneering efforts.

So many dear mentors, teachers, colleagues, and friends have encouraged and assisted my journey of promoting the resiliency message and have deepened my insight. A special thanks goes to Bonnie Benard, Emmy Werner, Peter Benson, James Hollis, William R. Miller, Gerald Zahorchak, Nancy LeBaron, Janis Kling, Bruce Trueman, Craig Noonan, Keri Starbuck, Donna King, Jan McBride, Constance Avery-Clark (and the rest of "Cadre One"—you know who you are). Finally, I am especially grateful for the years of support, encouragement, and priceless assistance from my brother Don Henderson, who never gives up on his sister.

Contents

1 You Were Born Resilient

People typically react with surprise and a certain amount of disbelief when I tell them, "It is more likely for someone who experiences great adversity to bounce back from it with a resilient outcome than not." I share this in the **resiliency** seminars that I have given to hundreds of audiences across the U.S. and in other countries over the past 20 years. I tell my audiences that in fact, resiliency, defined as the capacity to spring back, rebound, and overcome adversity, is "hard-wired" into the human makeup.

There is still a prevalent belief if someone is abused, traumatized, or stressed by severe crises, that person may not make it through this adversity, that he or she will be completely and permanently derailed by the experience. In reality, most people not only "make it through" but they go on to mine the life lessons of the difficulty. They bounce back smarter, stronger, and with the self-esteem of having accessed a core of overcoming they didn't know they had within them. The growing body of research from psychology, sociology, psychiatry, and social work that focuses on what happens to people over time that experience great adversity has yielded this knowledge. The outcome of this research has in fact coined a new concept: positive development from adversity.

So, why does the myth prevail that disaster leads to a destroyed life? Perhaps it is because our survival instincts, also hardwired into the human species, cause us to pay much more attention to the potential for life destruction than to the potential for overcoming, rebuilding, and transcending the negative. This is acutely obvious surveying the nightly news, or reading news reports online or in publications. The emphasis is on the negative, and the subtext is one of horrific, non-ending stress and floundering. Yet the thousands of stories in which people have done well in the face of awful life circumstances and experiences go unreported and unnoticed.

Resilient Every Day

In reality, all of us are resilient every day. Psychologists studying human reactions in the face of awful adversity (such as war, abuse, poverty, illness, and similar adversity) have concluded that we all have an innate, self-righting, and transcending ability. (Some of the research of these psychologists will be highlighted throughout this book.) Though we don't usually realize it, we access this resilient core daily in ways great and small such as when we lose our car keys or cell phone, or when the alarm doesn't go off, or when the washing machine breaks down, or we get lost driving to a new destination. Each day is filled with these types of incidents and each day is filled with our resiliency. Yet, it is something that we usually don't give a second thought to…we just cope.

You have probably picked up this book because you are going through something really difficult, not just the loss of keys or a cell phone. Someone very close to you may have died. You may be suffering terrible anguish because of a tragedy you have gone through. You may be trying to go back to school after years away or retraining for a new job because you are now unemployed. Or maybe you are still looking for work after years of trying. Perhaps you have been severely injured, emotionally and/or physically. Or, perhaps your adversity is a chronic challenge like Janine who has struggled throughout her life with depression, despite trying many medications. In addition, she has a stressful job in which she is undervalued and underpaid, is a single mom of two teens, and her ex-husband has never stepped up to support his children.

Or you may relate to Daren, who was devastated when after only a few weeks of marriage, he began having significant problems with his new wife, Kayla. They had dated a year and a half before the wedding and were doing fine, so he thought. But after he moved into her small duplex, two bedrooms and one bath for the couple and Kayla's teen-aged son, conflict developed. But Daren didn't really know what the problems were and Kayla wouldn't, or couldn't, tell him. He suggested counseling and she refused to go. A year later, Daren was divorced, depressed about it all, and still mystified. He determined, however, to learn from the painful experience. He went to counseling by himself, and read all he could about mid-life marriages, and what makes them work or falter. Years later, he still didn't understand Kayla, but he had become more aware of himself and the "red flags" he missed before the wedding. Death, divorce, disaster, destruction, on-going stress and challenges are a part of the life journey of being human, but so is the overcoming of them.

Strategies from Social Science Research

My guess is that you typically focus on the difficulty and pain of your problems, which is understandable. This book will encourage you to focus, in addition, on the ways you have and are—like Daren—maneuvering through, climbing over, outwitting, and accessing an innate core of yourself, your resiliency. And it offers strategies from the social science research that has looked at how people are able to bounce back from and transcend their difficulties.

You may also find in these pages a connection between this science and your unique philosophical or spiritual perspective. A group of Air Force chaplains who recently went through my resiliency training of trainers reminded me that a core Christian message is "The Kingdom of God is within." A Hindu man once handed me a note after a presentation with this quotation from the *Bhagavad-Gita*, the holy book of that religion: "Whatever is real, always was and cannot be destroyed." The Dalai Lama has said, "With realization of one's own potential and self-confidence in one's ability, one can build a better world." Resiliency researcher and professor Glenn Richardson has come to believe that the innate force that drives a person to a healthier, more self-actualized life can be called chi, spirit, God, or resilience.

One of my favorite inspirational authors, Wayne Muller, describes the universality of this "something" that is deep, wise, sustaining, and unblemishable in his book *How, Then, Shall We Live?* Noting that he is inspired by the scripture and sacred writings of "Judaism, Christianity, Buddhism, Sufism, Native American traditions, and others," he writes:

For thousands of years humankind has suffered famine, war, plague, hunger, and countless injustices; it has experienced numberless births and deaths. Each community of people has had to find some way to speak about [what] sustained them or brought them grace—even in the midst of terrible sorrow. We all struggle to name what cannot be named: the universal force that makes the grass improbably push its way through concrete, the force that turns the earth, the energy that blesses all life, the essential presence in our deepest nature that can never be spoken of with perfect accuracy.

Spirituality and Resiliency

Though the primary focus of this book is ways we are and can be more resilient as shown by the social science research, it is interesting to contemplate the alignment between the core belief in almost every spiritual tradition that there is something strong, wise, sustaining, and profound in each person and the research findings on resiliency. In this book:

- You will find ways you have already been resilient that you've never thought about before. And you will learn how to apply your resiliency in the past to current challenges.

- You will also learn how to take the findings of the growing body of research on resiliency, which has focused on how people overcome the most difficult life challenges, and apply these findings to your life and your problems right now.

- You will identify how to come out the other side of the difficulties of life stronger and wiser, i.e., your positive development from this adversity. And you will understand how this and other resiliency-connected strategies lead to **"authentic" self-esteem** vs. other less effective methods of self-esteem building.

- You will learn how your inner self is speaking to you and how to tune in to this voice of "inner guidance."

- You will also learn how to apply your research-based resiliency plan to whatever challenge you are facing now or may face in the future.

- You will take "The Resiliency Quiz" and be able to use it as a tool to measure your growing resiliency. And you will be introduced to other resiliency-building books, articles, and resources that I have found especially beneficial.

In this book, I am sharing with you all I have learned over the past 20 years about how to bounce back from life's adversity—no matter how painful—and to find the gifts of that adversity. I have divided each chapter into two parts: The first part provides information that I think is most useful and the second part—even more important to developing your resiliency—provides questions and activities so you can make the information *real for you*. In the back of the book you will also find a glossary of resiliency-connected terms that are typed in bold throughout the book.

Bouncing Back...Transformed

As you start this process, I want to emphasize that if you are so overwhelmed or distraught it seems impossible to understand or apply this information to your life, the most resiliency-building action you can take is to get some professional help. Counseling and therapy, especially by professionals who work from a resiliency/strengths-based perspective, will build your resiliency and help you to implement the strategies in this workbook. This workbook is not a substitute for needed treatment, and many resilient survivors of trauma note that counseling was the lifeline they needed in their darkest moments.

I spend time in my resiliency seminars convincing people that we are all "hard-wired to bounce back." I call attention not only to the growing body of research, but also to the many personal examples that all of us have seen in ourselves and in those around us. The whole of history in fact is one big drama of human overcoming; this is also the theme of great literature, cinema, and other storytelling throughout the ages. It's all about bouncing back, having been wounded, shifted, remolded, and transformed in the process. It's what we are born to do.

Making it Real for You

1. **Naming your resiliency in recent adversity**. Think of some small adversity you went through in the past day or two. Now identify, what helped you successfully manage and overcome that adversity? Think of both characteristics within yourself and anything or anyone outside yourself that helped.

   My grandma passing

   Eating lost of food

2. **Understanding the resiliency of someone you know**. Identify someone you know personally who has gone through and is "on the other side of" a very difficult life challenge. Write this person's name and his or her adversity [such as a experiencing a difficult divorce, dropping out and returning to school, losing a child or another close loved one, facing a severe illness, having a parent or spouse deployed in war, etc.]:

   Maddie   cancer.

   * How did this person "get through" this adversity?

     What *qualities* within this person helped him or her? *family*

     What *beliefs* held by this person helped him or her? *beeting cancer*

     Who helped them? *Doctors*

     How did they help? *medicine/sleep*

     What else helped? *Support*

* How have you observed this person using these same things in dealing with other problems?

* What else do you think would have helped him or her?

   friends/family

* What advice would you give anyone else facing this same type of adversity?

   stay strong

* What strength or life lessons has this person developed or learned from the process of encountering and going through this adversity?

   That life is never fair

3. **Connecting resiliency and your life philosophy.**

   * Do you have a life philosophy or spiritual belief that connects to results of psychological research on resiliency that show there is an "innate, self-righting, and transcending ability" within us all?

   Live Life how you want.

   * If so, what is it and how does it connect?

   * What is your reaction to the alignment of social science research on human resiliency and a common message in most spiritual traditions about a powerful, transcendent core of our being?

2 A Research-Based Plan for Overcoming Life's Challenges

The concept of human resiliency began trickling into academic research journals in the 1980s. Prior to that time, the primary emphasis of both research and practice in the mental health professions was on psychological damage. Psychology and psychiatry, still relatively new fields of social science, focused almost extensively on human problems and dysfunction rather than how people bounce back from them. The idea that children who experience great trauma would suffer life-long problems was strongly emphasized until a pioneering group of researchers began documenting human resiliency in the face of such suffering, and positive growth from such adversity. However, only in the past decade has the idea of "fostering resiliency" fully entered into the mental health professions, as well as education, community development, business, and the U.S. military.

Enlarging the Picture

Stephen and Sybil Wolin, a psychiatrist and a psychologist, describe several limitations of the traditional "damage" focus of psychology and psychiatry in their groundbreaking book *The Resilient Self: How Survivors of Troubled Families Rise Above Adversity* (published in 1993). They note that after being steeped in the "language of disease...and mastering an alphabet soup of symptoms and syndromes" mental health professionals "find illness and maladjustment" wherever they go. They add that the growing body of resiliency research points to the fact "we need to hear less about...susceptibility to harm and more about our ability to rebound from adversity when it comes our way." This of course does not mean that illness and maladjustment do not exist. But it does mean that the picture needs to be enlarged to include the enormous power of the human spirit to rebound.

As a newly trained clinical social worker working in a mental health agency in the late 1980s, I too focused entirely on stress, risk, and pathology. That was what I was trained to see and that was all I saw. I hadn't yet encountered the concept of resiliency or strengths in the face of adversity. Yet I observed that this exclusive focus on problems did not provide the empowerment and hope that is usually needed for someone to bounce back from the problems that brought people into our agency. I kept asking myself, "what is wrong with this picture?" as client after client left my intake assessments looking more discouraged than when he or she walked in. Intuitively, I was already sensing the limitations of the "damage only" approach and I was seeking another greater, and more effective-for-change, perspective. Fortunately, in 1990, I found research being reported in academic journals that talked about people being "far more than their problems" and evidence that all of us have "an innate, self-righting, and transcending ability."

A quick perusal of the past few years of resiliency research reports shows that the focus of this research has expanded from its early emphasis on the resiliency of children who experience great adversity to family resiliency, community resiliency, resiliency in all types of illness, resiliency and disabilities, resiliency and refugees, resiliency in every type of ethnic group, resiliency in incarcerated prisoners, resiliency in business, and resiliency in all aspects of military service, including war.

The Truth about Resiliency

An important outcome of the growing body of resiliency research is that it has identified the difference between those who experience great adversity and do integrate it, grow from it, and move on vs. those who are pulled down and derailed by it. Resiliency research points out:

- Resiliency is not something you either have or don't have. Everyone has the *capacity* for resiliency.
- Resiliency does not develop from internal traits only. Environments provide opportunities and supports that are as important, or even more important, than individual traits. Resiliency develops from an interaction between individual and environmental factors.
- "Gifts" emerge from the experiences of adversity (such as greater compassion, life appreciation and savoring, healthy reprioritization, empathy and a desire to be of service, a stronger spirituality, and self-esteem from having lived through a difficulty, to name a few).
- Resiliency frames a paradox that is true for everyone: Pain and wounds result from great adversity but so does positive human development and transcendence.
- It is possible to create in your life more of the conditions that have been shown to increase resiliency and thereby increase your capacity to move forward in the face of problems, grief, tragedy, and all types of human distress.
- You won't return to the "same normal" as before great adversity, but you can develop a new normal that includes a new way of looking at yourself, at your life, and at the world.
- Resiliency is a process over time. Often the bouncing back process is one of three steps forward and one or two back but the overall trajectory is one of overcoming and integration. This may take only a little time or it may take many years.

Damage vs. Challenge

A more accurate way of describing the journey through great adversity is suggested by the Wolins in their book. Rather than framing the aftermath of trauma, tragedy, or crisis as "damage," they describe it as a "challenge" suggesting a needed shift from the embedded "**damage model**" to a "**challenge model**" that recognizes each person has "a capacity for self-repair" and "strength can emerge from adversity." They emphasize this doesn't mean discounting real emotional pain: all of us should treat our pain, and the pain of others, with compassion and empathetic exploration. But in addition, we must also dig for and document the evidence of resiliency, including even small steps in the direction of successful overcoming.

Perhaps the single most well-known and acclaimed study of resiliency in the face of tremendous adversity is the Kauai study, which began in the 1950s, though results of the study were not published for many years. Pioneering psychologists Emmy Werner and Ruth Smith studied all the children born on Kauai in 1955 and followed them for several decades. They reported the results of the first decades of their study in their book *Overcoming the Odds: High Risk Children from Birth to Adulthood*. Of the 700 children in the study, of special interest was the one-third of this group termed "high risk at birth" because these babies had several risk factors. These risks included teen parent(s), parent(s) with addiction and/or mental health issues, living in extreme poverty and/or in situations of domestic violence, and/or receiving little pre-natal care. The remarkable finding was that by middle adulthood the majority of these "high risk babies" were living successful lives. Some showed early resilience while others floundered in adolescence, developing school, addiction, mental health, or criminal behavior problems. Yet eventually, the majority developed into competent and caring adults with the capacity, according to the researchers, to "work well, play well, love well, and expect well." This study provides an excellent example of the way the resiliency research challenges the idea that because you have had pain, tragedy and trauma in your life, you are doomed to a negative life trajectory. The exact opposite is shown in this study, and others like it.

The Power of Protective Factors

What is the process by which people, such as those studied in the Kauai study and other resiliency research, bounce back? Researchers have found people bounce back because of the power of **protective factors** (explained in detail in chapter three)—internal characteristics (many of which can be developed) and environmental supports/opportunities/conditions that facilitate resiliency.

Werner and Smith concluded in their book *Overcoming the Odds: High Risk Children from Birth to Adulthood*, protective factors "make a more profound impact on children who grow up in great adversity" than do "specific risk factors or stressful life events." In their later book *Journeys from Childhood to Midlife, Risk, Resilience, and Recovery*, they document that even most of the high-risk youths who did develop "serious coping problems in adolescence" staged a resilient recovery by mid-life. This landmark study, which spans more than five decades, describes ways in which resiliency requires environmental supports and opportunities and individual characteristics that propel individuals to accessing the opportunities and supports available.

In this way, internal and environmental protective factors work together in an interactive process. John, now a young man in his 20s, told a personal story of the interaction of individual and environmental protective factors in his early life, at a recent conference on resiliency:

When John was in grade school, his parents were barely making it on his dad's salary as a bus driver and his mom's income as a waitress. When he was in 5th grade, his mom died suddenly in a car accident, and the resulting emotional and financial devastation forced John and his father into a traumatic living environment. At the time he entered 6th grade, John and his dad were living in one room, and sometimes there was electricity and sometimes not, depending on if his dad had paid the bill. John's friend Glen convinced John to tag along to a new afterschool program that had been started as a pilot project in their middle school gym with limited grant funding. John realized from the first day in that program that he needed what was there: Caring, supportive adults, a safe and predictable structure, fun activities that also developed useful life skills, and nutritional afterschool snacks that could serve as dinner. (These were all environmental protective factors.) But John was not enrolled in the program and when he tried to get in, he was told by the director there was no more room. So, he drew upon his innate internal protective factors (which he didn't understand or name until many years later). He kept attending the program anyway despite being told that "there is no room" and one day he hung around so late, the director offered to drive him home. Not only did he accept her ride, but he had her come meet his dad, and when she saw his living situation she said to him, "John, I think we can find a spot for you in the program after all."

The program provided John with environmental protective factors he instinctively recognized from the first day he walked in would help him enormously. But John had to access several of his individual/internal protective factors in order to maneuver himself into a permanent spot in the program, including the perceptiveness/insight to immediately understand the program's value, self-motivation, persistence, and self-esteem (enough to let the director see how he lived).

In the next chapters you will learn how to grow the power of your individual and environmental protective factors. Increasing the power of these factors in your life is a central recommendation from resiliency research and it is something you can do...and must do, in order to increase the power of resiliency in your life.

More than You Realize

My guess, after having dialogued with thousands of people about this concept, is that you have more of both internal and environmental protective factors than you realize. The first step is to recognize your unique protective factors that are already operating for you, and the next step is to strengthen those and figure out how you can use them to bounce back from your current struggles. Then, you can set a goal of adding the power of more protective factors to your life… and this book will show you how to do it.

Making it Real for You

1. **Finding what has boosted your resiliency.** Think of a time you met a person or attended a new group meeting or found an organization that you instinctively knew you needed to boost your resiliency (even if you didn't know about resiliency at the time).

   ✳ Who was that person or what was the group or organization?

✳ What did you immediately sense you would get (that you needed) from continued interaction with this person or group?

✳ Did you get these things?
If so, how did they help you become more resilient?

✳ What personal qualities/characteristics did you draw upon to make sure you had continued access to this person or group?

✳ Did any more positive personal characteristics develop for you from this experience?

2. **Boosting your resiliency now.** What about *now?* Is there a person, group, or organization that you realize you need to connect with more *now* that would help grow your resiliency?

✳ Who is it or what group is it?

✳ What do you need to do to create a greater connection?

✳ What do you hope to gain that will help you *now* from this person or group?

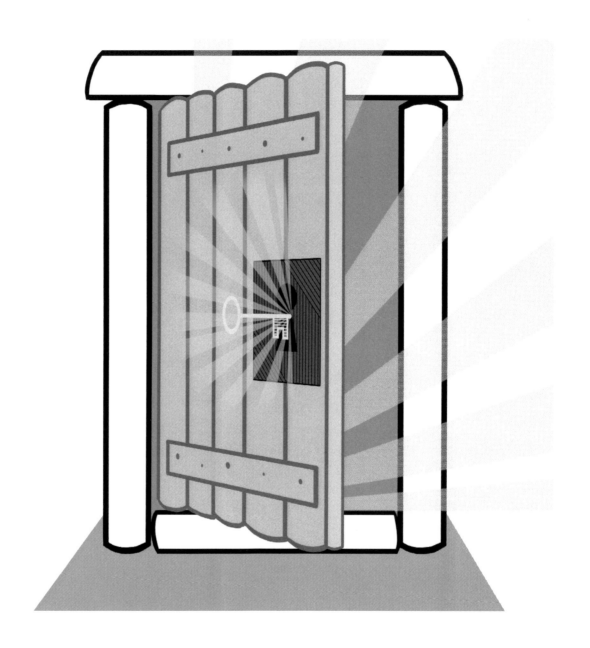

3 Unlock the Power of Your Personal Protective Factors

Protective factors? It is still a term that most people haven't heard of even though protective factors are the key to resiliency. I am somewhat amazed that after several decades of resiliency research, which repeatedly emphasizes the power of protective factors and protective processes, this term is not used in everyday conversations. It should be.

I have a fantasy of seeing a much more complete reporting of trauma and tragedy on the nightly news that includes not just the pain and suffering but the impact of a victim's protective factors. Such a report might sound like this:

"The victim of the robber's attack, fortunately, had a number of useful protective factors in her life that she drew upon right after the attack. She called 911 and then called her neighbor and both calls resulted in the arrival of immediate support. She used the self-calming skills she had learned in a stress-reduction class, which allowed her to provide a more accurate description of the attacker to police. She agreed to go to the hospital for a thorough check up and told the admitting nurse that she would follow through with counseling if she developed any sustained symptoms of **post-traumatic stress disorder** (PTSD). In addition, the victim asked another neighbor to install new locks throughout her home. These were her reactions right after the crime."

Post-Traumatic Growth

In a culture that fully embraced the reality of resiliency, a follow-up report on this crime victim might include her development of what psychologist Martin Seligman, a past president of the American Psychological Association, calls "**post-traumatic growth**." In his recent book *Flourish*, Seligman states, "The human species has evolved through millennia of trauma, and far and away the usual response to high adversity is resilience—a relatively brief episode of depression plus anxiety, followed by a return to the previous level of functioning." In addition, he reports, a substantial number of people, even those who do develop PTSD, "Then [begin to] grow. In the long run, they arrive at a higher level of psychological functioning than before." The victim of this crime, for example, might grow through pondering the motivations for the robber's actions and even work to forgive him. She might decide to volunteer at a crisis center to help other victims of violent crime. Or, she might realize there were subtle clues in her environment right before the burglary that she should have paid attention to.

Seligman's research has found, in fact, "individuals who'd experienced one awful event [such as torture, rape, death of a child, grave illness, etc.] had more intense strengths than individuals who had none. Individuals who'd been through two awful events were stronger than [those] who had one, and individuals who had three—raped, tortured, and held captive for example—were stronger than those who had two." Yet the concept of post-traumatic growth, like the concept of protective factors, is still relatively unknown.

Strength from Stress

Adversity, in fact, may be one of the best ways humans grow internal protective factors. As I often ask groups of foster youth, "What positive characteristics and strengths have developed in you that might not have developed if you had had an easier life journey?" I encourage you to reflect on the same question.

Protective factors do three things to promote resiliency:

- First, strong protective factors buffer some of the impact of negative life experiences. Shielding us against some of the impact, protective factors act as a safety net catching us before we slide into complete life disruption.

- Second, strong protective factors propel us through and over negative life experiences. Just like John, whose story is in chapter two, when faced with a crisis, tragedy, or trauma, strong internal protective factors assist us to grasp environmental lifelines.

- Third, internal protective factors offer evidence of our innate resilient core. Some of these characteristics may have been learned along the way, but our earliest memories of overcoming adversity (or our observations of young children) show evidence of being born with many resiliency characteristics.

   George, for example, remembered helping others who were distressed when he was in kindergarten, going over to comfort them. Jennifer recalled praying at four years old to her concept of God, even though she was raised without religious or spiritual training. Andrew remembered confronting a friend he knew was telling a lie when he was just five: Something in him perceived the falsehood. None of these people have any memory of being taught to engage these protective factors…at a time of stress or difficulty these qualities *just emerged*.

This chapter is about unlocking the power of your personal/ internal protective factors. (In chapter four, you will learn how to create a "wheel" of environmental protective factors.) The first step in unlocking this power is to see how your internal protective factors operate in your life. Working alone, with someone you love, in a group, or with a counselor, fill out the following chart and then do the other "Making it Real" activities.

Making it Real for You

1. **The Resiliency Chart**

Your name_____

List a major life challenge/adversity you have gone through	List all your personal qualities (internal characteristics) that helped you make it through this adversity—rack your brain, ask people who know you well, list as many as you can. (Be as specific as possible):
	List the environmental supports that helped you as well: Any person, organization, place, activity, etc. that assisted you

When people bounce back from adversity, one main reason is that the strengths (protective factors) on the right hand side of this chart pull them to a resilient outcome.

✷ How did your protective factors (written above on the right hand side of your resiliency chart) help propel you through your adversity?

✷ How did going through this adversity foster (or force) your positive growth, i.e., ways you became a better, stronger, or wiser person?

2. Using the List of Personal Resiliency Builders (Individual Protective Factors).

The personal characteristics and environmental supports you have listed on the right hand side of your Resiliency Chart are, in fact, your protective factors. I have compiled a list of the innate personal characteristics resiliency researchers have found help people bounce back from difficult adversity. This list, shown below, should be viewed as a *menu* not a check-list. In other words, no one has all of these developed in full, perfected manifestation. But everyone has some of them. Faced with a similar challenge, each of us may use the individual protective factors unique to us.

For example, if you are driving your friends to an important event and get lost, you might pull over to the side of the road and use your smart phone to figure out the route to take, using your self-motivation; or you might pull over and ask everyone in the car to help you figure out where to turn next, using the power of relationships with others. Or, you might suddenly notice a complicated road sign that you'd missed before (but you think has the information you need), using some perceptiveness. Each of these is an appropriate action to deal with the everyday adversity of getting lost while driving; no one is better than another, they are just different.

You can strengthen your personal protective factors by answering: Which of the following have you identified for yourself on the right hand side of your Resiliency Chart? (You may have listed yours using different words than those used below. See if your words are describing, in your own way, any of the following):

Personal Resiliency Builders
(as shown in the growing body of resiliency research)

Individual Protective Factors that Facilitate Resiliency

Relationships – Sociability/ability to be a friend/ability to form positive relationships
Service/Helpfulness – Gives of self in service to others and/or a cause
Life Skills – Uses life skills, including good decision-making, assertiveness,
          and impulse control
Humor – Has a good sense of humor, can laugh at difficult situations
Inner Direction – Bases choices/decisions on internal evaluation
          (internal locus of control)
Perceptiveness – Insightful understanding of people and situations
Independence – "Adaptive" distancing from unhealthy people and situations/autonomy,
          able to go your own way when you know it is the right way for you
Positive View of Personal Future – Optimism/expects a positive future
Flexibility – Can adjust to change; can bend as necessary to positively cope
          with situations
Love of Learning – Capacity for and connection to learning
Self-motivation – Internal initiative and positive motivation from within
Competence – Is "good at something"/personal competence
Self-Worth – Feelings of self-worth and self-confidence
Spirituality – Personal faith in something greater
Perseverance – Keeps on despite difficulty; doesn't give up
Creativity – Expressiveness through any type of artistic endeavor, and/or using
          imagination and creative thinking or other processes

✳ Write down the individual protective factors listed in the chart that are most natural for you, i.e., which ones do you use most frequently?

✳ Identify a personal problem or challenge you are now facing. How can you use your individual protective factors shown in the chart above to help you overcome, learn, and grow from this situation?

Recall the earliest time in your life you can remember using one or more of your protective factors. What are some early protective factors that you can remember using?

✳ How old were you at the time, and what was the situation?

✳ How does this memory give you clues to your resilient core?

3. Adding to your individual protective factors. Resiliency research is in its infancy, only a few decades old. Researchers are continuing to explore other personal characteristics that facilitate resiliency.

✳ What other personal characteristics within yourself or others can you add to the boxed list of individual protective factors?

✳ How do you think these characteristics increase resiliency (i.e., what is your rationale for adding them to the list)?

Select one personal protective factor from the boxed list (or from additional factors you have listed) to strengthen.

✳ What one have you chosen?

✳ How can you strengthen it? (Use your best ideas, or research how to develop this characteristic, and/or ask others you respect for their ideas.)

The Resiliency Wheel

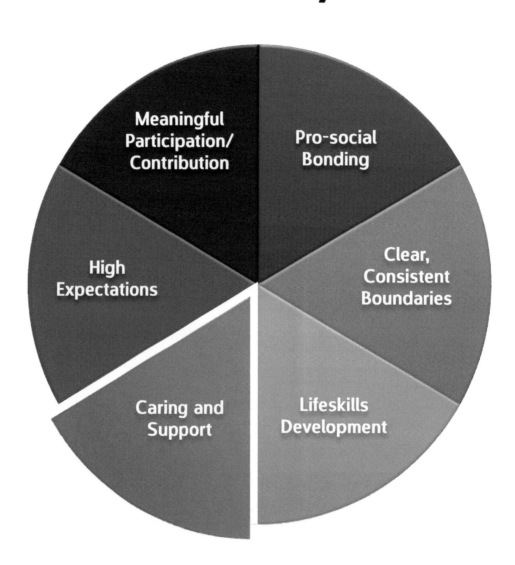

4 The Resiliency Wheel: Boosting Your Resiliency Every Day

You can create a circle of resiliency-building conditions in your life that I have named **The Resiliency Wheel**. It is a synthesis of environmental protective factors—external supports—that resiliency researchers have found are extremely powerful in helping people back from adversity. Living a life with these six conditions in place will help you bounce back from challenges, great and small. They act as a safety net to catch you when you experience difficulty; In addition, they form a wheel of support that helps propel you forward in taking necessary steps to achieve your life goals.

Basic Needs Across the Lifespan

One theory about these conditions is that they are actually basic human needs across the life span, that from birth to death everyone does better in environments that embody these factors. Research on the best schools in America (where attendance is high, academic achievement is high, morale is high, and the dropout rate is low) shows that these schools have a foundational **school climate** that provides these six conditions. A "positive school climate" is in fact synonymous with the conditions of the Resiliency Wheel. Other research on "the best places to work in America" conducted by *Forbes* magazine shows that in the workplace, too, people are the most productive, satisfied, and committed when they are surrounded by these six conditions.

The most powerful environmental protective factor is genuine caring and support in your life as highlighted on the Wheel. A nearly universal finding from resiliency research is that caring and support is the foundational environmental protective factor. The other five, in fact, emerge from this one.

The good news is that authentic caring and support does not have to come from a lot of relationships. In fact, one surprising finding from the resiliency research is the power of even one truly caring and supportive relationship in the lives of people who experience trauma or tragedy. Obviously, having a few such relationships is the ideal. Caring and support from a few close people in your life is the most important resiliency-building condition you can create.

You can be one of the providers of caring and support in your life by asking yourself such questions as, "What would be very nurturing right now?" "How can I best show compassion for myself?" Simply finding a good listening ear in someone who cares about you is extremely resiliency-building. Uplifting music, time in nature, or reading an inspiring book are all examples of ways to nurture yourself.

Caring
and
Support

One of the most important ways to provide caring and support for yourself is to monitor how you talk to yourself. This is a particular challenge for people who have been traumatized during childhood, because a child's natural reaction to being traumatized is to think, "I did something to deserve this." Parents' or other care-givers' cruelty or even simple neglect can develop in children inner critical voices that seem at times to scream messages of condemnation or failure. Experiences with the larger culture in which you have come to believe you have somehow failed to measure up to a cultural standard can also activate this severe inner critic.

Self-help strategies for "taming the inner critic" and cognitive behavioral approaches (that examine and then replace the automatic negative self-talk) can be very useful. Since negative self-talk is the opposite of true caring and support it depletes rather than strengthens the power of this protective factor.

One thing is certain: These voices are not an accurate assessment of who you are. Continuing through this workbook can help affirm, "what is right with you is more powerful than anything (real or imagined) that is wrong with you." I got this phrase from Jeremy, who told me about his journey through 17 foster homes as a child. When I met him, he was in college and considered himself very resilient. What helped him the most, he said, were caring individuals throughout his childhood that communicated this very thing: what was right with him was more powerful than anything that was wrong with him.

Making it Real for You

1. Strengthening the power of caring and support in your life.

* What are the qualities that describe for you someone who is truly caring and supportive?

* Who in your life provides this for you?

* Is there a way you can gain greater access to one or more of these supporters?

* Where could you find other people who could strengthen this protective factor in your life? (Think of groups, organizations, gathering places of all kinds.)

* What are steps you can take to create one more caring and supportive relationship in your life?

* How do you provide caring and support for yourself?

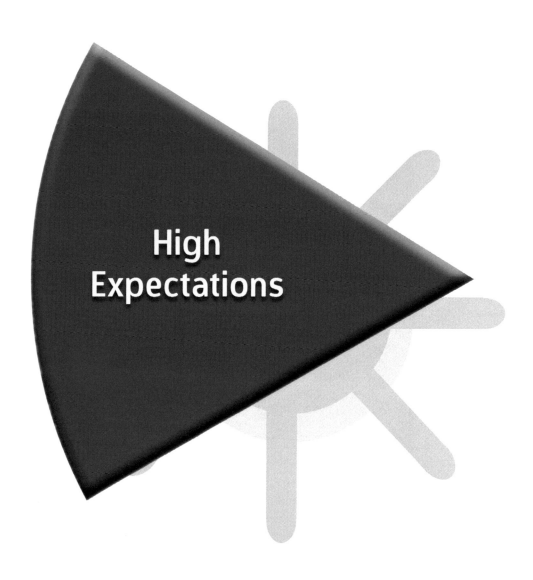

High
Expectations

People who receive the messages from others around them and from themselves, "I believe in you, I know you can make it" are more likely to bounce back from adversity than those who don't get these messages.

Psychologist Craig Noonan reports on research that has shown this in his article "A More Humane and Effective Approach to Motivating Change" published in the book *Resiliency In Action: Practical Ideas for Overcoming Risks and Building Strengths in Youth, Families, and Communities*. He describes "a classic study" in which alcohol counselors "were told psychological testing had identified some of their clients as having an excellent prognosis for recovery" when "in truth these clients were randomly selected from counselor caseloads and were no different from other clients." At the end of the treatment these clients were seen by their counselors as more involved in treatment and, in addition, actually had more positive outcomes than those who had not been given the "excellent prognosis." He adds, "The only difference between the two groups were the beliefs the counselors had in them."

In this same article, Noonan quotes addictions researcher William R. Miller as stating, "Given the right circumstances, [I believe] people will inherently choose healthy behaviors over unhealthy ones." A significant aspect of the "right circumstances" are circumstances in which people believe in you and express their belief that you can do what you set out to do and/or overcome whatever adversity you are grappling with.

The Pygmalion Effect

Educational research is filled with similar examples of these findings in a body of research that demonstrates "the Pygmalion Effect." The original research, conducted decades ago, was an experiment at an elementary school where students took intelligence pre-tests. Researchers informed the teachers of the names of twenty percent of the students in the school who were showing "unusual potential for intellectual growth" and would bloom academically within the year. Unknown to the teachers, these students were selected randomly with no relation to the initial test. When all the students were tested eight months later, they discovered that the randomly selected students who teachers thought would bloom scored significantly higher.

Study after study, including at the college level, has confirmed the original research, leading to the researchers' conclusion, "When we expect certain behaviors of others, we are likely to act in ways that make the expected behavior more likely to occur," as reported by the Duquesne University Center for Teaching Excellence (http://www.duq.edu/cte/teaching/pygmalion.cfm).

One middle school I worked with in Albuquerque, New Mexico several years ago changed its "Honor Roll" program to an "On A Roll" program in an effort to put into practice the idea that everyone can achieve greater success in the resiliency-building environment of "high expectations" for all. In order to be recognized as "On A Roll" students needed only to raise their grades one letter. Everyone who did this was rewarded as "on a roll" (which included an all-school awards assembly). A couple of the teachers in this school confided to me, "We were amazed at how many of our underachievers decided to participate and did well!" The fact the school made such a change communicated its belief that all students could be "on a roll" and the results validated the power of an environment in which people receive messages of high expectations.

Optimism and Health

A recent article published by the Mayo Clinic (http://www.mayoclinic.com/health/positive-thinking/SR00009) reported that researchers are continuing to explore the effects on health of positive thinking, i.e., optimism about one's ability to overcome adversity and about one's future. Benefits that these expectations provide may include:

- Better coping during hardships and times of stress
- Increased life span
- Lower rates of depression
- Lower levels of distress
- Greater resistance to the common cold
- Better psychological and physical well-being, and
- Reduced risk of death from cardiovascular disease.

As the Mayo Clinic article points out, it is possible with practice to shift to regularly communicating "high expectations" for yourself. And you can make a concerted effort to surround yourself with people and situations in your life that communicate their belief in you as well.

Making it Real for You

1. **Identifying environmental messages of "high expectations"** (adapted from the Mayo Clinic article listed above).

Negative messages (from others or from yourself)	Positive message that communicate "high expectations"
I've never done it before!	It's an opportunity to practice learning something new.
It's too hard.	Tackle it from a different angle. Break it into small steps. You can do it!
I don't have the resources I need.	Necessity is the mother of invention and you are a creative problem-solver.
I'm too lazy to get this done.	Let's re-examine some priorities. This is important and you can do it.
There's no way it will work.	You can figure out and take just the next step.
It's too big a change.	You can take a chance.
I'm not going to get any better at this.	You've learned other things that were hard at first. How did you do that?

* Who in your life gives you mainly messages that are in line with the right hand side of the chart?

* What other environments in your life provide you with these positive, high-expectation messages?

* Where could you get more of these messages?

2. Adding to your personal messages of high expectations.

* Choose one message on the left side of the chart that you typically give yourself. Practice replacing that message with the opposite one for one week. Write it here:

* Then do the same with another one.

* Identify a challenge you are facing right now. Write it down. List additional resources or supports that will help you meet this challenge successfully.

* Write your "oath" of belief in yourself that you can successfully navigate this challenge.

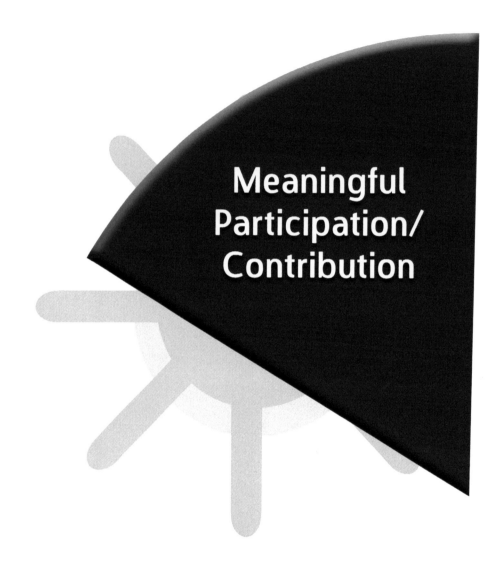

Meaningful Participation/ Contribution

Paradoxically, one of the best ways to bounce back from personal problems is help someone else with theirs. In addition, creating this protective factor in your life allows you to share your unique gifts and talents, which also builds resiliency. Professor Stephen G. Post, author of the book *The Hidden Gifts of Helping: How the Power of Giving, Compassion, and Hope Can Get us Through Hard Times*, detailed some of the research on the power of meaningful contributions to others in a recent interview. He said,

> I was struck by the 2010 Do Good Live Well Survey (www.VolunteerMatch.org) of 4,500 American adults. Forty-one percent of Americans volunteered an average of 100 hours a year. Sixty-eight percent of those who volunteered reported that it made them feel physically healthier; Eighty-nine percent said that it "has improved my sense of well-being"; Seventy-three percent said that it "lowered my stress levels." (Read the entire interview with Dr. Post at http://psychcentral.com/blog/archives/2011/05/28/helping-others-is-good-for-your-health-an-interview-with-stephen-g-post-phd.)

Post notes that social work research more than 50 years ago coined the term, "helper's high" and recommends that "we focus our efforts on some needful group that we feel called toward." Though most social science research has focused on the benefits adult volunteers receive, I have heard numerous personal accounts over the years of how volunteering also helps teens: A foster parent told me after one of my presentations that giving the 14 boys in his care the opportunity to serve disabled vets at the local community veterans' center did more for the boys than any other strategy he'd tried over many years as a foster dad. Suddenly, these boys were in a new, and very healing, role. They were now resources, rather than problems. This strategy, he said, was life changing.

The *"Helper's High"*

Allan Luks, former executive director of Big Brothers/Big Sisters of New York City and author of *The Healing Power of Doing Good: The Health and Spiritual Benefits of Helping Others,* has researched the "helper's high" phenomena over many years. Luks likens this high to that of a runner following a workout. He found evidence that helpers can even re-experience this high just by remembering their altruistic acts – even long after they take place. He notes in his book some of the most significant findings from his research:

1. The rush of euphoria often referred to as a "helper's high" after performing a kind act triggers the release of the body's natural painkillers, the endorphins. The initial rush is followed by a longer period of calm and improved emotional well-being.

2. Simply mentally recalling the helping act can cause the sense of well-being to return for hours or even days.

3. Stress-related health problems improve after helping others. These activities
    - Reverse feelings of depression.
    - Supply social contact.
    - Reduce feelings of hostility and isolation that can cause stress, overeating, ulcers, etc.
    - Decrease the constriction in the lungs that leads to asthma attacks.

4. Helping can enhance feelings of joyfulness, emotional resiliency, and vigor, and reduce feelings of isolation.

5. The awareness and intensity of physical pain can decrease while helping others.

6. Attitudes such as chronic hostility that negatively arouse and damage the body are reduced through acts of helping others.

7. A sense of self-worth, greater happiness, and optimism is increased, and feelings of helplessness and depression decrease through helping others.

8. When we establish an "affiliative connection" with someone (a relationship of friendship, love, or some sort of positive bonding), we feel emotions that can strengthen the immune system.

9. Caring for strangers leads to immense immune and healing benefits.

10. Regular club attendance, volunteering, entertaining, or faith group attendance is the happiness equivalent of getting a college degree, or more than doubling your income.

Staying Balanced

It is, however, important to stay balanced when pursuing this environmental protective factor. Make sure the good feelings that come from helping don't deplete your personal self-care. Feeling compelled to take care of everyone else first can cause you to overlook your own needs. As you build this environmental protective factor, consider:

- Are you feeling resentful towards those you are helping? (This is a clue that you need to rebalance your life so you are also nurturing your own needs.)
- Are you unable to manage your responsibilities and budget because you are giving so much? (Again, this is a clue to cut back, that your helping is out of balance.)
- Is feeling needed by others the *only* thing that makes you feel good?
- Do you say "yes" to helping someone when you really want to say "no"? (Learning to say no when needed is also an important environmental protective factor, which is covered later in this chapter.)
- Do you derive real joy from your helping? (This usually means you are contributing to someone or a cause that is truly important to you.)
- Are you able to contribute your unique talents, gifts, wisdom, and life experience in your helping activities?

Finally, one additional way to assess this protective factor in your life is to reflect on your family, work or school situation, and other places where you interact with others. Meaningful participation means that *your voice* and *your choices* are valued in these settings. Feeling disempowered, controlled, and disrespected any place in your life is the antithesis of building opportunities for meaningful participation for yourself. If this is the case, it is important to identify ways to increase the environmental situations in which you do feel your ideas and opinions are valued and respected.

Making it Real for You

1. **Identifying the opportunities for meaningful participation.**

   * Where do you volunteer/contribute in ways that are meaningful (important, potent, self-esteem building) for you?

   * What personal strengths/talents/qualities are you able to use in this contribution?

   * Are there others that you could share? If so, what are they?

2. **Increasing the power of meaningful participation.**

   * Are there other places/people/organizations that call to you as a place to contribute?

   * What are the barriers to you doing this?

   * Is your voice/choice respected at your job and/or school? If yes, how?

   * If no, do you need to change something about that situation so your voice and choice is heard and respected?   How could you do it?

3. **Achieving balance in contribution.**

   * Look over the bulleted list above and ask yourself the questions there. Are you out of balance in any way you can identify in your volunteering/contributing to others?

   * If so, how can you bring more balance into this aspect of your life?

Pro-social
Bonding

The protective factor of pro-social bonding is connected to the previous factor of opportunities for meaningful participation/contribution. Engaging in helping behaviors and contributions to causes and/or organizations that call to you strengthens pro-social bonding. This protective condition, however, also includes connecting to hobbies, developing talents, and learning about things you find interesting. Pro-social bonding means connections to any person, group, place, or activity (including solitary ones) that provides a positive (healthy) experience for you.

Taking care of and bonding with animals is one such resiliency builder. Time with animals has been shown to lower blood pressure, provide laughter and to even help people with various disabilities open up. Laughter provides many health benefits, so laughing with your pets is a great thing.

Bonding Benefits

People who are positively bonded to other people, animals, interesting activities, hobbies, and the development of their talents do better in life. ABC News summarized research on the multi-faceted benefits of engaging in activities/hobbies that give you pleasure. (Read the entire article at http://abcnews.go.com/Health/story?id=118258&page=1.)

The article quotes Professor Howard E.A. Tingsley, who spent 15 years researching the impact of engaging in "hobbies" on people of all ages. He interviewed 4,000 people in his research, and results were similar "for a variety of groups, from high school students to widows." In short, according to Tinsley, "People who were more active in leisure activities [including all types of hobbies such as sports, woodworking, gardening, reading, artistic and musical endeavors, cooking, crafting of all kinds, collecting, and bird watching, to name a few] reported greater satisfaction in life [and] they scored higher on standardized tests about satisfaction."

Tinsley said in the ABC article that we all need to get over any guilt about doing something interesting, rewarding, and fun, noting we are indoctrinated in this culture with a "Protestant work ethic" that views work as positive and leisure activities as not as good. However, research shows engaging in activities that give us arenas for expression, contribution, physical and mental exertion, affiliation, and just plain pleasure and joy is actually beneficial. What the hobby is doesn't matter; what does matter is that it be of interest and pleasurable and healthy for the individual. "It has to be intrinsically interesting; you have to have a certain amount of aptitude for it, yet also get some challenge from it." Tinsley added that a sense of control is important; people need to feel like they are making their own choices. For this reason, children and teens should be able to choose their own hobbies.

Finding "Flow"

Peter Price, a professor of internal medicine, describes the benefit of being totally absorbed in a hobby in the ABC article. Price is a rock climber because, he said, "it's a total escape from everything." He said he relates to what some psychologists are now calling "flow." This is "total absorption in what you are doing. You're free of self-consciousness. Whatever your hobby is becomes an end in itself and when you're into that state of 'flow' you're enjoying yourself."

Research on what prevents teenagers from engaging in drug abuse and other "high-risk behaviors" has shown that kids who are bonded to pro-social activities, such as positive hobbies, are less likely to try to find a "high" from potentially self-destructive behaviors. As Katie, a high school senior who had struggled with drug abuse told me after she successfully participated in a community dance recital before an audience of several hundred, "Who needs drugs? Dancing is my high!"

Making it Real for You

1. **Discovering "hobby" activities that give you "a natural high" as well as provide challenge, self-enjoyment, and satisfaction.**

   * What are these activities for you?

   * Describe how they benefit you:

   * What keeps you from engaging in these activities more often?

   * Can you think of ways to overcome these barriers?

   * What is an interest or talent you would like to develop into an active hobby in your life?

   * How could you do this?

2. **Strengthening other contributors to your environmental protective factor of pro-social bonding (including people, animals, groups, organizations, and positive places).**

    *   List all the other ways you can think of to strengthen this protective factor in your life:

    *   What is the next step you can take to make this happen?

3. **Identifying a time in your life when your positive connections (of any kind) protected you from engaging in an unhealthy response to stress or adversity.**

    *   What was the situation? Describe it here:

    *   What pro-social bonds protected you?

    *   How did they protect you?

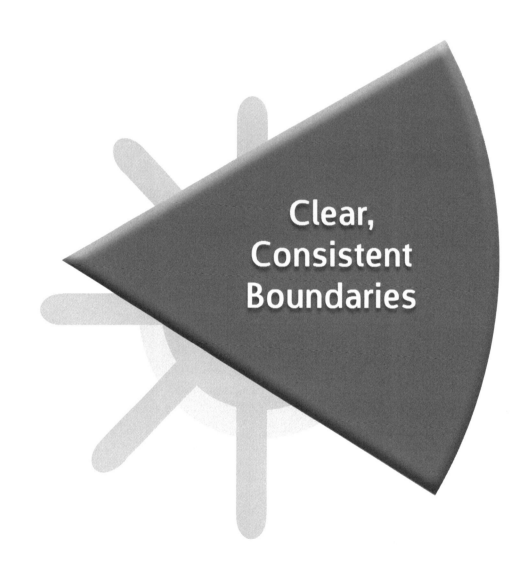

Clear,
Consistent
Boundaries

Feeling safe and respected, knowing what to expect, and avoiding feeling overwhelmed also builds resiliency. This means developing the ability to say "no" appropriately, to stand up for yourself when necessary, and to provide yourself with what you need to feel a sense of safety. Personal boundaries can be thought of as the physical, emotional, and mental limits you establish to keep yourself from being violated, manipulated, or overwhelmed.

Who You Really Are

Creating clear and consistent boundaries also means developing a sense of who you really are, what makes you unique. Allison is the mother of two teen girls, Darcy and Samantha, who are as different as two people can be. Darcy is a "girl's girl" who loves everything frilly, whereas "Sam" is a tom boy who wears t-shirts from her favorite concerts and army fatigues. Allison is wise enough to encourage each girl to be who she really is and doesn't try to force onto either of her children ways of being that don't fit the inherent nature of the girl.

Many people have some difficulty creating this protective factor in their lives. This can be because they were abused in some way as children and therefore grew up having their boundaries disrespected and even violated. Or it can simply be because all of us want to be "good to others" and fear that standing up for what is or isn't okay might hurt someone else's feelings or cause them to dislike us. As adults, even if we weren't abused, we might find ourselves in a family, romantic, friendship, or work situation where our boundaries are violated.

Alan wound up in this situation in a volunteer position. He was very devoted to a spiritual organization he believed in and would do any job, at any time, and also take the wrath of the organization's director when she didn't think Alan had done something just right. He volunteered long hours without appreciation and even endured being publicly embarrassed when his work was criticized in front of a group. This situation did not involve a physical violation of boundaries, yet because Alan did not assert what he would and would not do and how he would be treated by the organization director, his boundaries were being violated. Donna was in a similar situation when her son and daughter-in-law frequently dropped off their two young children without making a prior babysitting agreement with Donna. In addition, Donna's neighbor dropped by almost every morning and talked her ear off because Donna couldn't tell her "no."

Difficulty Setting Boundaries

These two typical examples show why setting boundaries are important and also how difficult it can be to do it. Alan was devoted to his spiritual home but was being used by those there who didn't respect him. Donna didn't want her grandchildren to think she didn't love them and didn't want to make an enemy of her neighbor, so she continued to allow her boundaries to be violated.

You can assess that your boundaries are being violated if you are feeling, in any relationship with another person, group, or organization physically, emotionally, or mentally violated; resentful or angry; manipulated or used; overworked; or overwhelmed with the demands of the relationship. You might also feel these emotions if you are being forced to do or be something that is not right for you.

Setting boundaries starts with becoming aware that you are feeling your boundaries are being violated. Then, remind yourself of the following to strengthen your resolve to set clear and consistent boundaries:

- You have a right to set personal boundaries, and you are in charge of what is okay and not okay for you.

- You must take responsibility for how you allow others to treat you.

- Other people's needs and feelings are not more important than your own.

- Defending your boundaries sometimes requires a certain amount of "selfishness" which is actually wise "self-care."

- You can learn to say "no" and it gets easier with practice.

- You are not required to justify the boundary that you set.

Signs you are not maintaining healthy boundaries include:

- Doing things that are against your personal values or rights.

- Giving without any limit to other people or organizations.

- Letting someone else define you.

- Not saying "no" because you feel guilty or anxious.

- Not speaking up when you are treated poorly.

- Accepting advances, touching, and/or sex you don't want.

- Intruding on others without making sure you aren't violating their boundaries.

The Power to Negotiate

Some boundaries are absolute ("I won't use illegal drugs") and some can be negotiated ("I can work this Saturday morning if I can take the following Wednesday afternoon off to attend my school's basketball tournament.") Your boundaries can be announced in advance in any situation, set in the moment, or negotiated. Janet Woititz and Alan Garner note in their book *Life Skills for Adult Children*,

> Your boundaries will frequently be tested. Some people won't
> take you seriously. They'll try to get you to give your boundaries
> up, to adopt boundaries that are "fairer" – to them. They'll try to
> wear you down by giving you lots of reasons why you "should"
> give up your boundaries. They'll try to make you feel guilty and
> to drop your boundaries so they can go back to using you.
> Because you are not used to having boundaries, you may well
> find it difficult to counter their efforts.

36

Woititz and Garner offer several useful strategies, including:

1. Call a "time out." For example, the next time Alan got a last minute call to do some job he might not want or have time to do, he can say, "Let me think about it and get back to you." This can give him some time to assess the situation, what he really feels, and to even practice how he can say "no."

2. Assertively say "no." You may be in the habit of saying, hesitantly, "I'd rather not" or "I'm not sure" which gives others a signal they can try to manipulate you or wear you down. But saying "no" or "no thanks" is definite. Stand up straight, look the other person in the eyes, and speak firmly. You might have to inwardly calm yourself by telling yourself you have a right to say no, but outwardly, stand your ground.

3. Say "no" but offer an alternative. Donna for example could tell her neighbor, "I don't have time to talk this morning but I have an hour tomorrow afternoon at four." She could call her son and tell him, "I love my grandchildren, but I can only babysit once a week and I need to give you my okay *before* you bring them over."

4. Practice saying "no" in unimportant circumstances. Tell an unsolicited sales caller, "No, I'm not interested." When a bank teller offers you 20s, say, "No, I would like 10s." Woititz and Garner note that gradually you will move from saying "no" to strangers to "no" to friends and family members—and in other close relationships when necessary.

5. Use the "broken record" technique. When dealing with someone who is badgering you and seemingly "just won't take no for an answer" simply repeat the same phrase over and over, no matter what the other person says. "No, I'm not interested" or "No, I can't go with you" are examples of such phrases. The technique works when you make sure not to get pulled into arguing, defending, or justifying your response. Whatever the other person says, you follow up with your single phrase of "no."

6. Deliver an "if…then" contingency. Keeping your statements as unemotional as possible, set your contingency in proportion to the behavior you want stopped. Examples include, "If you keep yelling at me, I will hang up" or "If you keep pressuring me about this, I will leave."

As you strengthen the environmental protective factor of setting clear and consistent boundaries, continue to remind yourself that you are in an improvement *process* and treat yourself with compassion along the way. You will find that as the power of this protective factor grows in your life, you will feel more self-respect, a healthier self-concept, less stress, and more balance in your life.

Making it Real for You

1. **Assessing your boundaries and strengthening your resolve.**

   * Look at the list above of signs you are not maintaining healthy boundaries. Check any on the list that apply to you. Identify one major sign in your life that your boundaries need strengthened:

   * Look at the list of reminders that can help you. Write down one or two of these reminders that you can memorize and say to yourself when you are in a situation of needing to set a boundary:

   * Describe one situation you are currently facing in which you need to set a better boundary:

   * What strategies from the list above might help you in this situation?

2. **Identifying barriers to and benefits of setting better boundaries.**

   * List the internal barriers you struggle with that keep you from setting clear and consistent boundaries in your life:

   * Now list the benefits you will experience as this protective factor gets stronger in your life:

3. **Creating your life with clear and consistent boundaries.**

    ✳ Use the space below to describe your vision of your life with healthy boundaries, include all your close relationships, your work or school, and other groups/organizations and activities:

    ✳ List the next steps you will take to make this vision a reality in your life:

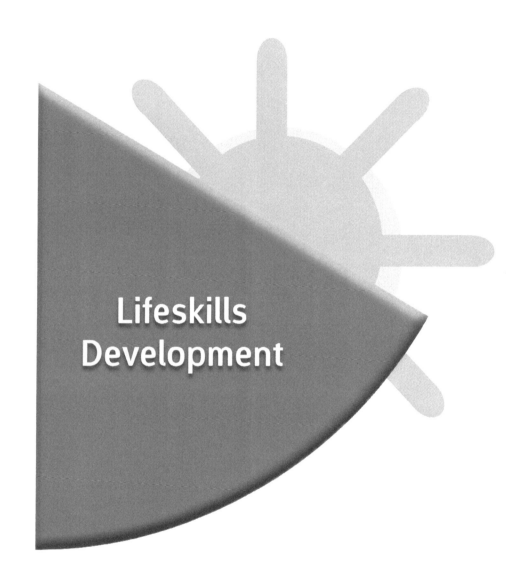

Lifeskills
Development

A new job or a new school, a never-before experienced problem or crisis, or a change in a relationship or a familiar role almost always requires new "life skills." Life skills can be divided into two categories. The first category is the social and emotional navigation skills, which have come to be associated with **Emotional Intelligence** (EQ) and **Social and Emotional Learning** (SEL). The second category is more job/school/task specific: How to write a resume, pass an exam, finish a report, or learn to snow board are examples of skills that fit into this category.

Defining "Emotional Intelligence"

The term "Emotional Intelligence" was popularized in the 1990s by *New York Times* science writer Daniel Goleman who became aware of decades of social science research that suggests people who can perceive, interpret, understand, and manage their emotions navigate better in life. In addition, people with high EQ are also better at empathizing with others and creating positive interpersonal relationships. Goleman and others have stated that a person's EQ is even more important than Intelligence Quotient (IQ) in doing well in life. There is controversy in psychology about how to best measure EQ and how to improve it, but it is generally thought that EQ develops over time and that it can be improved through education, training, and various types of counseling or therapy.

Goleman's culling of decades of research on social and emotional competencies resulted in his 1995 book *Emotional Intelligence*, which brought this concept into prominent focus. He outlines five crucial emotional competencies basic to social and emotional learning:

- Self and other awareness: understanding and identifying feelings; knowing when your feelings shift; understanding the difference between thinking, feeling and acting; and understanding that your actions have consequences in terms of others' feelings.

- Mood management: handling and managing difficult feelings; controlling impulses; and handling anger constructively.

- Self-motivation: being able to set goals and persevere towards them with optimism and hope, even in the face of setbacks.

- Empathy: being able to put yourself "in someone else's shoes" both cognitively and affectively; being able to take someone's perspective; being able to show that you care.

- Management of relationships: making friends, handling friendships; resolving conflicts; cooperating; collaborative learning; and other social skills.

Since the publication of *Emotional Intelligence*, K-12 schools across the country have been utilizing the body of research highlighted by Goleman's book to develop programs of Social and Emotional Learning. As Goleman reports on his website (http://danielgoleman.info/topics/social-emotional-learning), social science research over the past 15 years has shown the power of school wide SEL programs reinforced each year that teach children specific social-emotional skills like self-awareness, self-management, empathy, and cooperation. Such programs not only reduce violence, substance abuse, and other "risk behaviors"; this training also significantly improves academic achievement.

Improving Social/Emotional Functioning

Throughout our lives we can benefit from improving aspects of our social/emotional functioning. Here are some everyday strategies for developing this protective factor:

- Use a journal to increase your self-awareness and self-reflection, as well as a place to just "get it out"—all the anger, despair, or other emotions that are burdening you.

- Use "self talk" to encourage yourself (as detailed in the section of this workbook on "high expectations"). Writing down your self-encouragement is also powerful.

- Encourage friends, family members, and colleagues to tell you their points of view. Practice breathing and just listening to what they are saying, even if you disagree. Then, calmly state your point of view.

- Pay attention to and utilize specific strategies that are calming for you and that help shift your mood from negative to positive.

- Be aware of your "buttons," the things that automatically (and sometimes irrationally) make you angry and upset, and think about ways to deal with them.

- Find opportunities to cooperate and engage in collaboration with others. Notice the behavior of those in the group that is most useful and cooperative. Adjust your behavior appropriately.

- Strengthen your awareness of what feels okay for you and what doesn't and your ability to set positive boundaries for yourself (see recommendations in the section above on "clear and consistent boundaries").

- Set aside at least a few minutes of quiet, alone time every day to listen to your inner voice and become more aware of your social and emotional needs.

It is also important, of course, to figure out and acquire the more mundane skills we need to study, work, or enjoy other activities better. Our ability to do this successfully may even rest on our EQ competencies, since self-motivation and persevering are on the EQ list.

There are a number of books and courses that have been written to improve EQ. Many years ago, I facilitated groups based on the Janet Woititz and Alan Garner book *Life Skills for Adult Children*, which though written for grown children of addicted parents, has become my personal favorite practical resource for improving EQ competency. I think most people, teens and adults, could benefit from the very down-to-earth self-help offered by this book. It includes skills training in:

- Making contact with others (including making friends)
- How to (appropriately) express feelings
- Active listening
- Asking for what you want
- Solving problems
- Asking others to change their behavior(s)
- Handling criticism
- Establishing and defending boundaries
- Fighting fair
- Ending conversations, ending visits
- Ending relationships, and
- How to get started on any of this.

Finding a Counselor

I have emphasized earlier in this book my belief that in some cases, boosting your resiliency requires counseling, treatment, or therapy of some kind. I am restating that belief here: If you assess that you are experiencing long-lasting depression or rage that you feel you can't control or other emotions or behaviors that burden your ability to effectively function, nothing can take the place of a professional counselor who can coach you through the important journey of better managing these emotions or behaviors. When seeking a counselor or therapist remember you have the right and obligation to interview that person, asking all questions that are important to you, including: "Do you work from a resiliency/strengths-based perspective?" My recommendation is that you find someone, if you decide to go, that answers "yes" to that question.

Making it Real for You

1. **Informally assessing your EQ.**

   * Look over the first bulleted list above that summarizes five areas of EQ as outlined by Goleman. Circle one of the five that you are strongest in. Then, put a check mark by one you want to work on. Write it here:

   * Identify ways that you have tried to improve this life skill:
     Has anything helped you? At this point in this workbook, can you think of addition strategies to strengthen this area? What are they?

2. **Celebrating and strengthening your life skills.**

   ＊ Look over the list of life skills from the *Life Skills* book by Woititz and Garner. Circle one or more of these you are strong in. Then, put a check mark by one you want to work on. Write it here:

   (You may want to purchase this or a similar book, or attend a class, or simply go on-line for ideas about developing this life skill.)

   ＊ Write down a brief plan you will follow to improve this area of your life. Think about how you mastered something else you needed to learn that was difficult at first. What helped you in that instance? How can the same thing(s) help you in this situation?

3. **Considering the possibility of counseling or therapy.**

   ＊ Have you ever considered getting counseling or therapy to better manage an emotional or behavioral aspect of your life?
   Have you gotten it?

   ＊ If you think it would be beneficial, write down any barriers in your mind to getting therapy:

   ＊ If applicable, answer this question: "Could I try counseling or therapy for four or six weeks to see if it helped?"

4. Identifying other types of life skills to help you at work, school, or for fun.

* Think about your work situation and/or your school situation. Can you identify a work or school-related skill that would help you?

* Write down your ideas for how you can develop this skill? (For example, think of anyone you know who could mentor you, any workshops you've seen where you can learn it, or books or online resources that might help.)

* Is there a fun activity or hobby that is calling you? What is it?

* How can you develop the skills you may need to participate?

5 Who (and What) is in Your Mirror?

The idea that each of us develops a self-concept based on "**mirroring**" messages we receive from our environments is described by psychiatrist Stephen Wolin and psychologist Sybil Wolin in their book *The Resilient Self: How Survivors of Troubled Families Rise Above Adversity*. They connect this concept of the "mirroring" in our lives to resiliency. They write:

> According to child development experts, we are all born without any idea of who we are. We piece together a picture of ourselves—first of our bodies then of our essential nature—by seeing our reflection in the faces of the people who take care of us. Children who generally see love, approval, pleasure, and admiration in the mirror of their parents' faces construct a corresponding inner representation of themselves that says, "I am lovable. I am good." In troubled families [or in the environments of other troubled caregivers] the mirroring process goes awry, and children are at risk of forming an inner representation of themselves that says, "I am ugly. I am unacceptable."

The Power of One "Believing Mirror"

The Wolins discovered in their research, Steve's with adults raised in addiction-plagued families and Sybil's with children who struggled in traditional schools, the power of even one positive "alternate mirror." This is someone who provides you with mirroring in which "you can see a more pleasing [and accurate] image of yourself," that has the power to break "the spell" of unlovability cast by troubled caregivers. Such people, according to the Wolins, are the most powerful protective factor you can have in your life.

All of us benefit from filling our lives with "believing mirrors" including, as the Wolins also point out, the believing mirror we provide for ourselves. They share the example of a young man who walks out of a family fracas, goes to the garage, fixes a bicycle, and says to himself, "I am competent." They note that the pleasing self-images you can collect by surrounding yourself with people in your environment who mirror belief and support for you, as well as your own positive self-mirroring, "accumulate over time" and add to your resiliency.

I believe the dynamic of being negatively influenced by the "mirrors in your life" to dislike and disrespect yourself can happen even if you didn't have an unusually troubled family. Beth was raised in a family where she felt wanted and loved. Yet she married when she was just 19 and her youthful naiveté prevented her from seeing the warning flags that she was marrying an abusive partner. Her husband never physically hit her, but he criticized and condemned her constantly, including demeaning her frequently in front of their daughter. It took many years for Beth to wake up to the fact she was being emotionally abused. The impact of the negative mirroring she got from her husband took its toll and she felt worse about herself year after year. Eventually, though, the alternate mirroring messages from close friends and family members, who saw what was happening to Beth and told her she deserved to be treated better, helped Beth to actually leave. Her own internal protective factors of perceptiveness (which emerged over time), motivation, and spiritual faith which were never extinguished by her husband helped her as well.

Our culture as a whole does not often provide "a positive, believing mirror." Even when we are raised in loving families, the cultural messages of ways we don't measure up to an unattainable ideal can take their toll. It is important to ask, "Who is in my mirror? What messages do I most regularly get from the people around me?" Messages of support that focus on a belief that what is right with you is more powerful than anything that might be "wrong," increase resiliency. Messages that criticize or condemn tear you down instead.

"People are Contagious"

Psychiatrist Daniel Amen, a neuroscientist and brain researcher, notes in his book *Healing the Hardware of the Soul: Enhance Your Brain to Improve Your Work, Love, and Spiritual Life*:

> People are contagious. Who you spend time with matters.
> When you are with positive, supportive, and loving people, you
> feel happier and more content, and you live longer. This is not
> only intuitively true; research has demonstrated it again and again.

If you have experienced a lot of trauma, abuse, and/or tragedy in your life it can be tempting to assume that "God" or "Nature" or the "Universe" is somehow punishing you or condemning you or that you don't deserve happiness. "Why me?" you may cry out in distress. Some of the most helpful advice I ever received was, "Instead of asking, 'why me?' ask, 'what is Life calling you to do in this moment?'" In other words, accepting the resiliency premise that positive growth can blossom in great adversity, know that at the very least you can use the adversity to learn and grow.

Jade, who has had breast cancer three times, adopted this attitude. Though she went through days where she was despondent, throughout her journey she kept asking, "What can I learn from this? What am I being called to do with this situation?" In the process of this inner questioning, she eventually decided that she wanted a completely different career than what she had chosen; accounting "did not really feed my soul" she said. "I want to train to become a family counselor." She reprioritized her life in other ways as well. "Before my last bout of cancer, I wouldn't travel much or do things just for me. Now I know I want to live life to the fullest and explore places I have never been. And I am going to do it!"

Jade's story connects to another important aspect of mirroring: Make sure that the person you see when you look in a mirror is the person you truly are. Psychologist Carl Jung believed that the most important purpose of life for everyone is to be who they are, unique from everyone else. He called becoming your true self the process of

individuation. Ignoring, repressing, and denying who you really are and what you really need, according to Jung, results in psychological and/or physical distress. It is a temptation most of us are faced with regularly: In Jade's case, become a counselor, which was Jade's heart's desire, or follow in her father's footsteps as an accountant, which she was pressured to do? Blindly accept the cultural norms for your gender or step out and do what you are called to do, regardless? Accept the invitation to the Friday night cocktail party, or take the time to go on a solitary hike in the forest, which is what you really need? Over and over again we have the choice to do and be what really calls to us, or to do what someone else wants for us.

Jungian psychologist James Hollis gives some guidance about how to discern the "right" direction for your life in *What Matters Most: Living a More Considered Life*. Noting how easy it is to be influenced away from who we truly are by those around us, he recommends considering if a particular calling or enthusiasm "occasion[s] a *resonance* within us." He explains,

> *Re-sonance* means to "re-sound," to set off echoes within us, to perseverate within as a tuning fork hums long after it is struck. Whenever we experience resonance, something continues to hum for us....Every one of us at some level knows what we want to do, need to do, have to do to live our lives.

Looking for Resonance

Looking for resonance, which may require solitude to mull which direction your truest self longs for, is one way to assist your process of individuation. So is examining your experiences of jealousy or envy. Rather than pushing these feelings away, it is useful to consider if the person you feel jealousy or envy towards is living out something that calls to you, too. Dreams, fantasies, and strong (sometimes illogical) pulls to a particular person, place, or activity all need to be attended to, according to Hollis. That part of you that "knows at some level" may have trouble breaking through your conscious, rational mind, so messages may come in seemingly irrational ways that need to be sorted out.

Hollis notes we must live our lives by finding "what feeds us." Then "having been fed, [we] share our gifts with others...healing, satisfaction, and meaning only come when we identify what [feeds us], and find also the courage and the wherewithal to make it happen." Most great leaders, cultural heroes, artists, and creators of all kinds are people who are highly individuated, comfortable with "marching to their own inner drummer." Doing so, however, can take a lot of courage and is also frequently uncomfortable. If we choose comfort, resisting the continuous urge from deep within to shift, grow, and blossom throughout life, life often loses its luster. People who choose this route may become depressed or confused or cynical. So this choice, too, ultimately causes discomfort. Hollis gives another piece of advice about how to discern the best way to go: If you are at a crossroads and don't know what decision to make, choose the route that will expand your life and express your uniqueness rather than the route that is safe, comfortable, but ultimately stifling.

In *How, Then, Shall We Live,* Wayne Muller offers a wonderful story that is a metaphor for the process of individuation:

> My friend Michael told me that as an activist in the civil rights movement, he and his friends were regularly arrested and put in prison. Many were imprisoned illegally, simply as intimidation for their beliefs about justice and equality. Whenever they were in prison, they would sing. The guards would come and yell at them and sometimes even beat them, demanding they stop. They felt the prisoners' songs were dangerous. And in a way they were right: The singing insisted there was a more potent truth than jail or oppression.

Your individuation is your song. Others around you, including the conditioning of the culture, may attempt to get you to stop. Becoming who you really are can be dangerous to those who want you to be who they think you should be or for a culture that resists positive change. Keep singing.

Making it Real for You

1. **Identifying your mirrors.**

   * As a child, what type of mirroring did you get, according to the Wolins' explanation above?

   * How has this mirroring helped you or wounded you?

   * Who, in your life right now, is a "positive, believing mirror"?

   * How can you access others who provide this for you?

   * What kind of mirroring do you provide for yourself?

2. **Evaluating your individuation.**

   * Describe a recent situation in which you expressed who you really are (your beliefs, values, opinion, needs, etc.) despite what others thought:

* Can you identify with Jade's story of extreme adversity as a "wake-up call" that she needed to live her life very differently?
  Have you ever gotten a similar "wake-up" call?

* If so, what was it?

* Think about a recurring dream, fantasy, or constant yearning you feel in your life. Can you identify what it might be trying to tell you?

* Overall, do you think you are generally "true" to who you really are, i.e., do you sing "your unique song"?

* If not, what blocks you from honoring the "call" of your individuation?

* What can you do to be more in alignment with your real self?

3. **Hearing the inner "resonance."**

* What is your reaction to Hollis' concept of deep listening for an inner resonance in deciding what paths to take in your life?

* Have you had this type of experience? What was it?

6 The Resiliency Route to Authentic Self-Esteem

A controversy has developed about what is known as the "feel-good only" approach to building self-esteem because of follow-up social science research on the impact of this approach. This research has shown that making yourself feel "special" by using methods such as just affirming "I am somebody," doesn't do any good, and may do harm. As I reported in my article "The Resiliency Route to Authentic Self-Esteem" in the book *Resiliency In Action: Practical Ideas for Overcoming Risks and Building Strengths in Youth, Families and Communities*, researchers say that one result of the affirmation-only approach to building self-esteem is a "counterfeit positive self-assessment" that can set people up for disappointment in the "real world." This may be especially true for young people, who develop an unrealistic opinion about their specialness only to be disillusioned "when life's inevitable disappointments present themselves." This "feel-good only" self-esteem deflates when it encounters disappointment because it is not based on something that is solid and real. You have right now in your life the ingredients of real self-esteem. This chapter explains how you can identify these ingredients and use them to create a foundation of authentic self-esteem.

To build solid, real self-esteem people of all ages need what I call "the resiliency route to authentic self-esteem." This type of self-esteem is not the mere fluff of meaningless affirmations. It is based on recognizing actual accomplishments, as well as identifying, understanding, and using your strengths, and living a life filled with expressions of your unique talents and gifts.

Doing As Well As You've Done

Acquiring this authentic self-esteem starts by shifting your internal focus for yourself—and for others, including children—to a thorough appreciation and application of how you (or they) have "done as well as you've done." The first step on the resiliency route to self-esteem is to believe the resiliency research: everyone, of all ages, has an innate capacity for bouncing back *and has already demonstrated it countless times in their lives.* The second step is to identify your personal patterns of this bouncing back. Specifically, instead of asking yourself why you aren't "doing better" ask yourself, "How have I done as well as I have done?" This question can't be emphasized enough. For some people, just getting out of bed each morning and pushing through the day is a success. However you are doing, you could be doing worse, e.g., missing more work, skipping more school, feeling more depressed, eating or drinking even more. So, how are you doing as well as you are doing? What internal characteristics or environmental conditions keep you from being "farther from the bottom" than you are?

A few years ago, I was training a group of community social workers in Sacramento, California. Tom was one of them, and when I asked the group to focus on one client they were especially worried about, Tom said, "The boy I chose to focus on is at rock bottom." I said, "Really? What is his situation?" Tom said, "He is living in the fields outside of town." Tom went on to explain that this boy was a homeless teen living in agricultural fields in the area. I said to Tom, "Well, that's terrible. We want him out of the fields. How long has he been out there?" Tom answered, "A few weeks." I said, "I wouldn't last a few nights living in the fields," and I repeated, "We want him out of the fields." I added, "I want you to list all the characteristics of this boy's life, within him and in his environment, that are helping him survive in the fields. Those are his resiliency builders right now. Let's start by identifying and strengthening those."

Identifying your personal resiliency building protective factors (in chapter three) and working to strengthen your environmental protective factors (in chapter four), including contributing your gifts, talents, and energy to others is a foundation for authentic self-esteem. These characteristics exist within you and within your life and they are far more real than simply affirming that you are special. (Indeed you and everyone else *are* special in unique ways, but just saying that, without tying it to anything that is a reality in your life, does not provide the solid foundation of authentic self-esteem you need when the going gets tough.)

Practice giving yourself (and others) credit for what you/they have gone through and overcome—especially for the inner strengths, talents, skills, and personal characteristics used to do it! Even if you currently face a terrible problem, suspend focusing there, and take some time to thoroughly assess and appreciate what you have already accomplished in overcoming other difficulties. Then, ask of yourself (or someone else): How can your strengths be used to overcome current life challenges?

A Powerful Approach

This is a powerful approach. A high school counselor told me recently how she applied it. A student in her school, Sandy, was referred to this counselor because she was failing in two subjects, math and science. Normally, the counselor told me, she would immediately confront a student with the problem—in this case two failing grades—after making some brief small talk. Instead, after the small talk, the counselor opened her session with this question: "Sandy, I have learned a little about your life. Tell me, how have you managed to do as well as you have done?" Sandy, the counselor reported, immediately burst into tears and said, "Never in all my years has anyone acknowledged what it has taken just to get to school." Most of the rest of the session was spent identifying all the strengths Sandy had used to "do as well as she had done." Towards the end of the session, the counselor said, "Let's talk about how you can use all these strengths you have shared to bring your grades up in math and science."

For the last 40 years The Gallup Organization has been conducting research into the best way to maximize a person's potential. Findings from this research have been reported in several books, including *Now, Discover Your Strengths* by Gallup executives Mark Buckingham and Donald Clifton. Two of the findings Buckingham and Clifton report are "each person's talents are enduring and unique," and "each person's greatest room for growth is in the areas of his or her greatest strengths." Another conclusion of the Gallup Research: "The real tragedy of life is not that each of us doesn't have enough strengths, it's that we fail to use the ones we have." I would add a second tragedy, connected to the first: We obsess about our imperfections and weakness, and we fail to recognize as well as underestimate the power of our strengths.

Admittedly, using the resiliency route described here is not always easy to do. As I pointed out in chapter one, our culture is obsessed with "what is wrong." We internalize this and it is difficult not to dwell on what is wrong—with our bodies, our homes, our leaders, our financial status, our material accumulation, and our children. And we are very specific in naming all that is wrong: "My thighs are too fat," "My carpets are dirty," "My income is too low," or "You are too lazy," "Your room is too messy." Rarely is anyone as constant and specific in giving oneself or others the credit that is due.

The approach I am suggesting here does not mean ignoring real problems—such as alcoholism, other self-destructive behavior, or an abusive, violent temper. But the resiliency route to authentic self-esteem does mean:

- Giving yourself (and others) credit for all that has been overcome, all the ways you/they have demonstrated resiliency. This includes naming these accomplishments and the strengths as specifically as possible. Practicing naming strengths for others can sometimes make it easier to do this for yourself. And naming others' strengths often creates more optimism—for you and the other person.

- Focusing on how you (or others) have done as well as you/they have done.

- Identifying other strengths—important lessons learned, virtues, talents, skills and capabilities, how you help or serve others, all the best things about being you.

- Maximizing these strengths and using them to solve current life problems.

Stop Hiding Strengths

The final step on "the resiliency route to authentic self-esteem" is finding ways to live in your personal strengths and ways to use them to the utmost. "Too many individuals hide their 'sundials in the shade'," conclude Buckingham and Clifton. I can attest to this fact after training thousands of people in naming their strengths. Over the years, I have observed an almost universal hesitancy.

You may believe, as many do, that naming your strengths and talking about them will cause others to think you are arrogant or bragging. In reality, most arrogance is the result of people not realizing and owning their strengths, therefore feeling "less than" others. They may compensate for this feeling by acting arrogant or by (often unwarranted) bragging. When you, and others, can truly live in the solid knowledge of your personal strengths, arrogance or bragging is not needed. Furthermore, you won't be threatened by someone else's success when you can easily claim your own.

Buckingham and Clifton recommend that instead of obsessing about correcting all the (real or imagined) weaknesses, people should put their strengths to work. They advise, "Become an expert at finding and describing and applying and practicing and refining your strengths." The happiest and most productive individuals are those who do just this, states psychologist Martin Seligman in comments about the Buckingham and Clifton book that are printed on its back cover. In addition, social scientists are finding that the healing of serious mental illness and addiction is more likely to occur through therapies and programs that focus on clients' strengths. (This information is shared in chapter eight.)

More Motivation

"People are more motivated to change when their strengths are supported," notes social work professor Dennis Saleebey, editor of *The Strengths Perspective in Social Work Practice*. I agree. People I have interviewed who have left gangs, recovered from alcohol and other drug addiction, made it successfully through college despite a childhood of abuse, or overcome other significant traumas have told me the same thing. Over and over, I have heard that success in overcoming serious challenges happened because people came to truly believe "what was right with them was more powerful than anything wrong" and they finally were able to acknowledge and more consciously use all their strengths.

Making it Real for You

1. **Identifying and building on how you have "done as well as you've done."** Think of an on-going challenge in your life (such as maintaining a healthy weight, getting to work or school on time every day, getting enough exercise, dealing with life-long depression or anxiety, or some other long-term challenge). How have you "done as well as you've done"? What qualities within yourself, as well as outside supports, have helped you "stay as far off the bottom as you are"? List these, being as specific as possible:

   * How can you grow these qualities and strengthen these supports?

   * What stands in the way of you giving yourself credit for "doing as well as you've done"?

2. **Identifying and growing other strengths.** List your other strengths that have helped you through life challenges including important lessons learned in your life journey, virtues, talents, skills and capabilities, how you help or serve others, all the best things about being who you are:

   ❋ Which of your strengths can help you with a current life problem?

3. **Living in your strengths.** What would you answer if you were asked in a class or seminar to "name your strengths"?

   ❋ How would you feel publicly answering this question?

   ❋ How can you change any feelings of discomfort in naming and talking about your strengths?

   ❋ Determine to stop denying your strengths. Practice saying, "Thank you" when your strengths are acknowledged in any way.

   ❋ How do you react to the assertion "people are more motivated to change when their strengths are supported" quoted above?

   ❋ How can you become the number one supporter of your strengths?

   ❋ How do you think this will improve your self-esteem?

7 Listen Within: How to Find & Follow Your Accurate "Gut" Guidance

When I tell people I am currently researching intuitive guidance and its connection to resiliency, almost everyone has an **intuition** story they are eager to share with me. They usually describe a time when sudden or strong intuition saved themselves or someone they love from tragedy or propelled them to an unexpected good fortune. In my own journey of resiliency, developing strong intuition has been invaluable.

Carrie, a social service agency worker and mother of three, told me about the time she was on vacation with her sister, who agreed to take Carrie's young children down to the hotel pool while Carrie went out shopping. Carrie showered and got ready to head out. But Carrie could not go to her car and leave. Something—and like most people, Carrie had a difficult time describing that something—insisted that she go down to the hotel pool instead. This was totally irrational; Carrie completely trusted her older sister to look after her children. Fortunately, Carrie followed the "gut" feeling that something was wrong. When she got down to the pool, she couldn't see her youngest daughter, just seven years old. Frantically circling the pool, she finally glimpsed her daughter's hot pink bathing suit below the surface of the water. It had gotten caught on a loose drain at the bottom. "Mommy," her daughter sputtered after Carrie quickly pulled her out of the water. "I couldn't speak but I was calling and calling you!"

Intuition Changes a Life and Changes the World

My friend Alicia, a middle-aged widow wanting to remarry, told me about a life-changing intuition that occurred when she was completely burned out with online dating. Alicia had been trying the online route to finding a new mate for about a year but dates with every "lead" had been uncomfortable, unsuitable, or downright rude. She decided she'd had enough and that she wasn't going to meet anyone else listed online. "But," she told me, "I remember exactly where I was standing in my dining room when I heard in my heart something like a voice, but it wasn't an audible voice, say to me: 'Just meet one more.'" She already had planned a meeting with Matt, who was going to drive from a city two hours north to have lunch with her the following week-end. Alicia followed her intuition and didn't cancel on Matt. Their meeting turned out to be "love at first date" for both of them. Within a few months, they were engaged.

Steve Jobs is an example of someone whose intuition changed the world. Jobs traveled to India and integrated some of the ways of the East into his life, including developing the power of intuition. Jobs is quoted as saying in his official biography published shortly after his death, "I began to realize that an intuitive understanding and consciousness was more significant than abstract thinking and intellectual logical analysis." He also said that "intuition is a very powerful thing, more powerful than intellect, in my opinion. That's had a big impact on my work." His intuitive sense, which he clearly welcomed and honored, is obvious in Jobs' incredible ability to foresee—and then design—what users would want next.

Psychologists are increasingly studying the universal human experience of intuition, focusing on the power of the **unconscious**. "The unconscious being excavated by scientists [today] processes data, sets goals, judges people, detects danger, formulates stereotypes and infers causes, all outside our **conscious** awareness," writes Sharon Begley, a science reporter, in *The Wall Street Journal*. (Read the entire article at http://online.wsj.com/article/0,,SB103064467423376915.djm,00.html.)

She continues, "In fact, there is a growing consensus that the unconscious is a pretty smart cookie, with cognitive capacities that rival and sometimes surpass that of conscious thought. How smart is the unconscious? [Recent] experiments probing the power of intuition [have] sold me."

In one study Begley describes, volunteers got faster and faster at pressing the "correct" buttons on screens divided into quadrants. They'd been told to press the button that matched where an X appeared. But after awhile, they began anticipating the X's appearance correctly. They couldn't verbalize this. They just seemed to know intuitively what was going on. In another study, Begley reports:

> Researchers …at the University of Iowa had volunteers draw from four decks of cards. Each card was marked with an amount "won" or "lost." Two decks had big wins and losses and, if played consistently, yielded a net loss; the other two had smaller wins and losses and, over time, returned a net gain. Almost all the volunteers learned to avoid the risky, losing decks, though as in the game of X's, none could articulate why the losing decks gave them a bad feeling. But if the conscious part of their brain was confused their body was not: choosing from the losing decks increased skin conductance, which measures minute levels of sweat and correlates with stress.

Different Ways of "Knowing Truth"

Researchers hypothesize an unconscious part of ourselves picks up on and stores huge amounts of information our conscious mind misses. Other preliminary findings: people solve problems better after sleep than subjects who focus continuously on the problems; relaxed mental states fosters this kind of 'offline' problem-solving; and defocused attention contributes to flashes of insight.

Psychologists William R. Miller and Janet C'de Baca have been researching this phenomena—sudden flashes of insight—for more than a decade. They have published their amazing findings in *Quantum Change: When Epiphanies and Sudden Insights Transform Ordinary Lives*. Their research focused on 55 individuals from completely different backgrounds who had such profound intuitive experiences their lives were

60

transformed in some healing way. The researchers conclude the foundational lesson from their study is "*there are different ways of knowing truth.*" They go on to explain:

> The scientific method, for example, is a useful and valuable tool for discovering truth. It was through careful observation and logic that thinkers like Nicolaus Copernicus and Galileo Galilei came to be convinced of new truths that contradicted shared certainties of their day. To claim that this is the *only* way of knowing, however, is to ignore experience… [As] Carl G. Jung described [there is] an intuitive way of knowing that matches well the experience of [the] quantum changers [in our study].

Intuition can be cultivated and developed. Here are some ways:

- Still your logical mind in ways that work for you. Meditation is one way, but so is spending time in nature in a solitary, reflective activity.

- Keep an intuition journal. Highly intuitive people, like the people studied by Miller and C'de Baca, speak of feeling a strong, certain, peaceful *knowing* that occurs beyond the logical mind. Write down when you have such knowing. Then check it out; discerning accurate intuition is a learning process over time.

- Listen to unusual signals from your body—a bad feeling in your gut, for example, or an expanded feeling in your heart about something or someone. Research confirms our bodies can know things our minds do not comprehend.

- Keep track of your dreams. Pay particular attention to recurring dreams, which may have a message from your unconscious. Remember that the language of dreams is the language of metaphor. Dreaming about a big, new, black sports car, for example, probably doesn't mean you should go buy that car. Instead, ask yourself, "What does the image of this car (or any other image in your dream) mean to me? What is my unconscious trying to tell me by using this image?"

- Engage in activities that activate the "right side of the brain" such as music, dance, art, or other forms of creativity.

Assessing Your Intuition

What are some clues that what you perceive as "intuition" is off-base? If you find your "intuition" is condemning, controlling, or directs you to do something illegal or immoral, realize that inner sense is not true intuition. People I have talked with who have spent years developing their intuition report this aspect of themselves brings them greater health (including avoidance of a tragedy), peace, guidance in decision-making, and unexpected "blessings." Maria, for example, told me, "I will be in a situation and I'll have a sense about what should happen or what seems like the right step…It's just a certain inner knowing that I feel…a truth I feel about something. I don't know how I know, but I feel lucky, fortunate, and blessed to have this in my life."

Making it Real for You

1. **Discovering your intuition.**

    ✳ Have you ever had an experience of certain knowing without knowing how you knew, which turned out to be correct? If so, describe it here:

    ✳ Why do you think your intuition was activated in this situation?

    ✳ What, if anything, have you done to strengthen your intuition?

    ✳ Has it worked?

2. Strengthening your intuition.

 ❋ After reading the list above, what resonates for you as a way you can strengthen your intuition?

 ❋ Choose one thing and try it for at least several weeks. What is it?

 ❋ Who can you talk to about your experiences with intuition?

Prochaska and DiClemente's Six Stages of Change

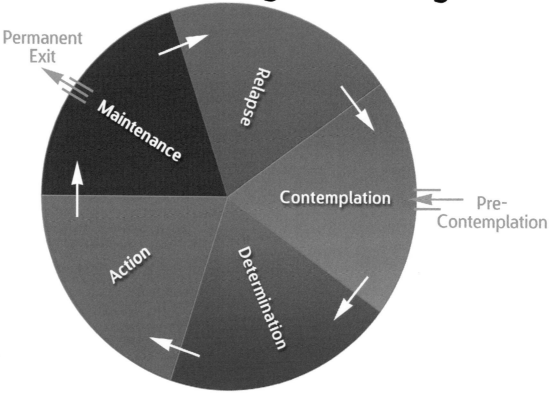

8 Identify Your Achilles Heel (& Stop it From Tripping You Up)

I didn't understand for a long time that mythic stories throughout different cultures are expressions of the whole of human experience with hidden meanings that are usually as helpful today as they were centuries ago. I used to find mythology irrelevant to my life. Many myths, however, point out timeless truths. The myth of Achilles is a story with a deeper meaning applicable for all of us.

Achilles was a powerful Greek mythological warrior. Though he had the great courage, fortitude, and strength of a noble fighter—attributes he no doubt developed with much discipline and effort—he had one unresolved weakness that eventually led to his complete downfall. According to the myth, as a child his mother dipped him in the river Styx, which had magical powers that would protect him from the vulnerabilities of war. She held him by the heel with her thumb and forefinger, leaving just one small area vulnerable to attack. Though he became a brilliant warrior, alas, a fateful arrow struck Achilles in the heel. Achilles went down and no one could save him.

Avoid or Conquer?

Thus, the term Achilles heel was born. In spite of overall strength, an Achilles heel is a sole weakness that can lead to failure or downfall. An Achilles heel is an aspect of yourself that holds you down and holds you back. You may spend a lot of your life working to overcome, or at least successfully manage, this aspect of yourself…or you may try to avoid it, which is by far the more dangerous attitude. If you know what your Achilles heel is, then it loses some of its power to trip you up because you are on the lookout for it, and can outsmart its potential to completely derail you. If you don't see it or don't deal with it, it has far more power.

I believe living a resilient life involves becoming aware of and dealing with anything with the power to undo your life. Perhaps the best example of this is addiction. Addiction, especially alcohol or other drug addiction (but also gambling and other addictions) can eventually completely undermine every other part of someone's life. Uncontrolled anger, spending, lying, or any criminal behavior can do the same thing.

So, do you have an Achilles heel? The first step in overcoming or successfully managing this aspect of yourself is to look at it straight on with the certain knowledge that you have "an innate, self-righting, and transcending ability"—your resilient core, a driving force that wants you to be healthy. A clue as to what your Achilles heel might be is the level of defensiveness you feel when someone or some situation shows you in some way that you may have this weakness.

Brian grew up in a home with two alcoholic parents. His childhood was filled with constant physical and emotional trauma, chaos, fear, and uncertainty. Despite that, he had demonstrated a lot of resiliency, though his constant self-criticism got in the way of him recognizing this fact and acknowledging his strengths. He had started smoking as a teen but he kicked the habit in his 30s. He also struggled with alcohol abuse, but was able to manage his drinking so it didn't overtake his life. One of the reasons he could do this, he said, is that he was determined not to be an alcoholic like his parents since he had seen what that addiction did to their lives. And he thought he had succeeded.

But when Brian was in his late 30s an attractive girlfriend who was addicted to OxyContin, the prescription painkiller, threw a fateful arrow that hit Brian's Achilles heel. Brian had stopped smoking and controlled his drinking, but still hadn't recognized or dealt with early wounds and patterns unconsciously impacting his life: his low self-esteem, negative self-talk, lack of self-nurture, and social isolation. These remnants of the early negative mirroring Brian had experienced left him susceptible to the lure of another drug that provided an escape from unhealed psychological pain. He began using the OxyContin with his girlfriend; he wound up addicted, and he didn't want to look at it. His rationale was, "It's just a prescription. And I am *not* an alcoholic!"

The Power of Acknowledgment

Rebecca struggles with an Achilles heel less toxic than drug addiction, though it has wrecked some havoc in her life. The good news is she recognizes it, accepts it as something she has to deal with, and even blogs about it:

> I'll be the first to confess that the Achilles heel I live with is perfectionism. I want everything done just right—right down to the last detail. I say that I live with it because I am honest enough to admit that I haven't overcome its grip in my life, particularly in business. Because I've acknowledged it as a weakness, I am able to keep an eye on it and easily recognize when it rears its ugly head. When I find myself getting too bogged down in the "nitty gritty" details in my life or work, my Achilles heel "meter" goes off, which prompts me to delegate this aspect to someone else, while I stay focused on the big picture (http://ezinearticles.com/?Keep-an-Eye-on-Your-Achilles-Heel&id=3119141).

Ironically, one debilitating Achilles heel is constant self-criticism and over-focusing on what you think is "wrong" with you. Successfully overcoming your Achilles heel involves acknowledging this aspect of your humanness and then dealing with it with equanimity rather than condemnation.

The first part of the journey to overcoming or at least managing your Achilles heel is to integrate into your life the strategies in this workbook. When you truly *know* your strengths, your capacity for resiliency, and "what is right with you is stronger than anything that might be wrong," you are better prepared to deal with your Achilles heel. The best route I have found for the journey of overcoming an Achilles heel is mapped in a research-validated process developed by psychologists James Prochaska and Carlo DiClemente called the "**Stages of Change Model**."

Stages of Change Model

As psychologist Craig Noonan writes in "A More Humane and Effective Approach to Motivating Change" published in the book *Resiliency In Action: Practical Ideas for Overcoming Risks and Building Strengths in Youth, Families, and Communities*, "this model describes six stages of change that have been identified in research" initially used with smoking and other addictive behaviors. In recent years, the model has been applied to weight loss, developing physical fitness, maintaining health (including medical compliance), and many other behaviors. The stages, representing a developmental process of change, are: 1) Precontemplation; 2) Contemplation; 3) Determination; 4) Action; 5) Maintenance; and 6) Relapse.

A precontemplator is someone who is not even considering the possibility of change and would probably be surprised or even upset if you suggested it. These are people often labeled as "in denial" about their problem, but as Noonan notes, "in fact they are more often just lacking in problem recognition…information that would allow them to evaluate their behavior and conclude that there is a need for change." Are you in the precontemplation stage? No, because the fact that you are reading this shows that you are already ready to consider that you may have a problem that is an Achilles heel for you.

Contemplators are ambivalent about change. They need to process their ambivalence in a safe and nonjudgmental arena. Confrontive counseling and treatment approaches, according to this model, can be counterproductive and create resistance to change in the contemplator. That is why looking at your "resistance" to something you think you might need to change is a great clue. But, Noonan notes, "Research has [shown] that empathic methods are more effective in creating a situation where clients can talk themselves into change." So facilitating your change with self-compassion and empathy is important. When your intrinsic motivation to change emerges, it is far more likely you will be successful in the long run. This motivation leads to the next stage.

In the determination stage you have made the decision and commitment to change and you begin looking for ways to do so. You may find these ways personally or seek the assistance of a counselor. A good counselor can share expertise on the ways that have proven most effective for others making similar changes and assist you in choosing what you think will work best for you. But you can also find the help you need in this stage in support groups, classes, and/or reading all you can find on how to make this change.

In the action stage you are engaging in change behaviors. This is where you will need all the support discussed in this workbook. Support is the key at this stage of the change process. Support should include encouragement and assistance in problem solving major roadblocks or setbacks.

The maintenance stage is very much like the action stage except the changes being made are broader life-style changes that will support the specific behavior change made during the action stage. These changes might be a new social support system, new health care behaviors, a change in employment, and so on. Such changes also may require assistance with accessing resources, problem solving, and general emotional support. Noonan says, "The idea is that they will create a life rich in rewards and low in stress so that the chances of a return to the old behavior (such as alcohol or other drug use) are minimized."

Trying Many Times

The last stage of change is that of <u>relapse</u>. It is included as an integral part of the change process. Prochaska and DiClemente found that people making changes often must go through the stages of change several times before they successfully complete the change process. During each cycle they generally do a little better. This fact is very important because it normalizes and destigmatizes relapse. Noonan observes:

> One of the most difficult parts of making a change is how to think about and deal with a relapse to the old behavior. When someone on a diet eats a piece of cake that is not part of his or her diet plan, the person often feels like a failure, that they have "blown" the diet. When someone feels like a failure it is difficult to continue with a change plan and it is often abandoned. In fact, the dieter has not "blown" the diet; he or she has just had a piece of cake. The most important [thing here is to focus] on the success that [you] have had, to problem solve what caused the relapse and how to deal with it in the future, and to get back to working the change program you have designed.

He adds, "The resiliency literature has identified [protective] factors in the lives of individuals that appear to protect them from the development and persistence of negative behaviors." He explains, "The negative behaviors either never develop or they are changed to more positive ones more rapidly than with individuals whose lives lack these factors." This emphasizes that strengthening your protective factors is a foundation for success is dealing with your Achilles heel. Using the stages of change model with compassion and determination, realizing you may go through the process outlined many times in the course of your change—and that is typical—is the best route I have found to effectively deal with whatever the challenge of your Achilles heel presents for you.

Making it Real for You

1. **Naming your Achilles heel.**

   * Do you suspect or know you have an "Achilles heel"? Is so, what do you think it is?

* What are the "clues" you have gotten from other people or situations in your life about your Achilles heel?

* How has this problem adversely impacted you or derailed your life?

2. **Applying the Stages of Change Model**.

* Looking at the stages of change model, what stage are you in?

* What do you need to move to the next stage?

* What are the barriers to you progressing in your change process?

3. **Managing your Achilles heel.**

* How have you managed or worked to overcome your Achilles heel in the past?

* What else do you think might help?

* Where can you get what you need?

4. **Dealing with relapse.** Another way to think of relapse in the process of change is a reversion back to an earlier step in the Stages of Change Model.

* Have you experienced a relapse in dealing with your Achilles heel?

* If so, what contributed to the relapse?

* Were you able to move back up the stages of change model again to a place of successful action and maintenance?

* What helped you do this?

* How does it help you to know that research shows most people go through the stages of change model several times before they are completely successful in making a difficult change?

9 How to Keep Going When the Going Gets Tough

It's one thing to read this book, it's another thing to be able to remember and use the strategies when you are severely stressed, depressed, or discouraged. Here is a brief summary, which I've called, "the four most important steps to fostering resiliency," to remind you of the most important resiliency-building strategies. If the going is tough right now you are probably feeling anger, anxiety, grief, or other intense emotions, which is understandable—these are normal reactions to a really tough time. While it's important to vent, don't get stuck: read these steps and then answer the question: What is the next step I can take right now, this moment or in this hour? Tomorrow, ask yourself the same question, and use an "inner mantra"(repeat to yourself),"Right now, I just have to take the next step."

The Resiliency Attitude: A Foundation

1. Surround yourself with "**The Resiliency Attitude**." — The first "protective" strategy is communicating to yourself and being around others with the attitude, "You have what it takes to get through this!" Remind yourself, "What is right with me is more powerful than anything that is wrong." It can also help to remember that spiritual traditions and resiliency research all point to an innate resilient core in each person, which sustains us and propels us throughout our lives.

2. Adopt a "**Strengths Perspective**." — "The keystone of high achievement and happiness is exercising your strengths," rather than focusing on weaknesses, concludes resiliency researcher and psychologist Martin Seligman in writing a review of the book *Now, Develop Your Strengths*. I recently asked a group of teenagers and adults to identify their strengths. Both age groups were at a loss–neither group could name strengths, and both were hesitant to share out loud even tentative ideas about what their strengths might be.

It is crucial that you remember your strengths. Right now write down all the qualities within yourself that have helped you deal with tough challenges in the past.

3. Create for yourself—and your family and support systems—all elements of **The Resiliency Wheel** listed below:

- Provide Caring and Support. Ask yourself, "What would be very nurturing right now?" "How can I best show compassion and caring for myself?" Often simply finding or providing a good listening ear is extremely resiliency-building. So is uplifting music, time in nature, or reading an inspiring book. Providing yourself and others with unconditional positive regard, love, and encouragement is the most powerful external resiliency-builder.

- Set High, but Realistic, Expectations. Effectively using this strategy involves identifying and supporting steps in the right direction rather than demanding instant perfection. Review the list of "high expectation messages" in chapter four. Make sure you are giving yourself these messages and are around others who do this for you as well.

    Ask yourself, "Do I need to give myself more high expectation messages right now?" and, "Who can I talk to who believes in me?"

- Engage in Meaningful Participation/Contribution to Others. This is one of the best ways to overcome a tough time in your life. Find someone or some group that can use your help and in a balanced way, give what you can. This often leads to a better perspective on your own challenges. Life is filled with challenges and everyone experiences them.

    In the wake of the 9/11 tragedies, a consistent message of psychologists interviewed about how to get through that time was, "Make a positive contribution in some way. Give whatever you have to give."

- Increase Positive Bonds and Connections. People who are positively bonded to other people (through a network of friends and family and/or clubs or organizations) and to enjoyable activities do better in life. This fact has been documented extensively by psychological and medical research. Reaching out to connect with someone, some group, or some activity that is positive is another strategy to successfully cope with adversity. Ask yourself what you can do today that is something fun, enjoyable, and that either utilizes/develops a talent or provides a positive social connection—or both.

- Set and Maintain Clear Boundaries. Feeling safe, knowing what to expect, and not being overwhelmed also builds resiliency. This means developing the ability to say "no" appropriately, to stand up for yourself when necessary, and to create for yourself a sense of safety. Setting and enforcing clear and consistent "family rules" as well as work, school, or other organizational policies are part of this process.

    Ask yourself, is there a boundary you need to set that will help you get through this tough time? Maybe you need to let something go to give you the energy to deal with your challenge(s). Maybe you are overworked, overstressed, overwhelmed. Set the boundaries that will help.

- Develop Needed Life Skills. Stress management skills, good communication and listening skills, healthy conflict resolution skills, and knowing how to assert yourself appropriately are some of the life skills needed every day. Right now ask yourself, "What life skills that I have can I use here?" or "What new life skills do I need to learn?"

Time to Become Resilient

4. Give it Time. — A resilient outcome requires patience. A few years ago, I interviewed Leslie, a young woman then 16 years old who had just finished the ninth grade on her fourth try. I asked Leslie how she was able to finally get through ninth grade. Leslie shared the two main reasons she had made it: First, her single-parent mom refused to give up on her, even during the years she was skipping school, using drugs, and lying. Second, the small alternative school her mother eventually found for her embodied the four steps outlined here. "Where would Leslie be if she hadn't had at least one person who stuck with her until she finally got through ninth grade?" I thought. Once again, I was reminded of the resiliency research message of the power of even one positive, believing mirror in the life of someone who is struggling.

Stories like this one have convinced me not to give up–on myself, on children, on my friends and family going through hard times.

Making it Real for You

1. **Identifying the next step.**

   * Write down the next step you need to take as you continue on during this tough time in your life:

   * Commit to telling yourself, "I just need to keep taking the next step."

2. **Discovering what life is calling you to do.**

   * Rather than dwelling in "why me?" questions, ask, "What is life calling me to do in this situation?"

   * Remember that your greatest growth may come out of this tough time. What was another tough time you went through that you now recognize also produced in you more strength, compassion, and/or life wisdom?

3. **Using The Resiliency Wheel.**

    ✳ Review each of the six aspects of The Resiliency Wheel. Write your answers to the questions listed in The Resiliency Wheel review above:

    ✳ What strategies from The Resiliency Wheel will help you now?

4. **Considering a counselor or therapist.**

    ✳ Ask yourself, "Do I need to get additional support" from a counselor at this time? Realize that the answer is definitely, "yes" if you are considering harming yourself or someone else, or are so overwhelmed right now that you cannot manage your life.

    ✳ If you think talking to a counselor might help you get through this tough time, what is the next step you can take now to find a counselor?

    ✳ Remember to ask potential counselors if they work from a "strengths-based, resiliency" framework.

5. Seeking spiritual support.

* Ask yourself, "What can I do now that feeds and calms my spirit?" (Some examples are spending time in nature, reading classic poetry, praying, meditating, journaling, or doing yoga.)

* If applicable to you, remember a time when spiritual support of any kind was useful for you. What was that support and how did it help? Can you access it now?

Nothing assists resiliency and overcoming as much as positive connections. In his book *Love and Survival: 8 Pathways to Intimacy*, cardiologist Dean Ornish describes in detail the astounding benefits of these connections. He cites decades of research that indicates feeling close, connected, loved, and supported lowers depression, anxiety, the incidence of heart disease, infections, hypertension, and even cancer. In addition, finding support from religious or spiritual beliefs also increases health. The single most important resiliency-building step you can take is to increase positive connections in your life: to people, animals, organizations, satisfying hobbies and activities, and/or to a spiritual path that calls to you.

10 The Resiliency Quiz... & Other Resiliency-Building Resources

I developed this quiz for anyone—teens, adults, elders—to assess and strengthen the resiliency building conditions in their lives. Use it for yourself or use it as a tool to help others you care about build their resiliency. One option: fill out the quiz before you read the workbook. Then, fill out the quiz after you have completed the workbook to see what has changed.

The Resiliency Quiz

by Nan Henderson, M.S.W. (reprinted from www.resiliency.com)
© Resiliency In Action, Inc. (Copies can be made for educational purposes.)

Part One:

Do you have the conditions in your life that research shows help people to be resilient?

People bounce back from tragedy, trauma, and stress by having the following "protective" conditions in their lives. The more times you answer yes (below), the greater the chances you can bounce back from your life's problems "stronger and smarter." Doing that is a sure way to increase self-esteem.

Answer yes or no to the following. Celebrate your "yes" answers, then decide how you can change your "no" answers to "yes." (You can also answer "sometimes" if that is more accurate.)

1. Caring and Support

__yes__ I have several people in my life who give me unconditional love, nonjudgmental listening, and who I know are "there for me."

__yes__ I am involved in a work, school, faith, or other group where I feel cared for and valued.

__no__ I treat myself with kindness and compassion, and take time to nurture myself (including eating right and getting enough sleep and exercise).

2. High Expectations

__no__ I have several people in my life that let me know they believe in my ability to succeed.

__yes__ I get the message "You can succeed," at my work or school.

__no__ I believe in myself most of the time, and generally give myself positive messages about my ability to accomplish my goals and/or overcome adversity.

3. Opportunities for Meaningful Participation/Contribution

__yes__ My voice (opinion) and choice (what I want) is heard and valued in my close personal relationships.

__no__ My opinions and ideas are listened to and respected at my work or school.

__no__ I volunteer to help others: a person, a group or a cause in my community, faith organization, or school.

4. Pro-Social Bonds

__yes__ I am involved in one or more positive after-work or after-school hobbies or activities.

__no__ I participate in one or more groups (such as a club, faith community, or sports team) outside of work or school.

__yes__ I feel "close to" at least some people at my work or school.

5. Clear and Consistent Boundaries

__yes__ Most of my relationships have clear, healthy boundaries (which include mutual respect, personal autonomy, and each person in the relationship both giving and receiving).

__no__ I experience clear, consistent expectations and rules at my work or in my school.

__yes__ I set and maintain healthy boundaries for myself by standing up for myself, not letting others take advantage of me, and saying "no" when I need to.

6. Life Skills

__no__ I have/use good listening, honest communication, and healthy conflict resolution skills.

__no__ I have the training and skills I need to do my job well, or the skills to do well in school.

__yes__ I know how to set a goal and take the steps to achieve it.

Part Two:

People also successfully overcome life difficulties by drawing upon internal qualities that research has shown are particularly helpful when encountering a crisis, major stressor, or trauma. The following list can be thought of as a "personal resiliency builder" menu. *No one has everything on this list.* When "the going gets tough" you most likely have three or four of these qualities that you use most naturally.

It is helpful to know which are your primary resiliency builders; how have you used them in the past; and how can you use them to overcome the present challenges in your life. You can also decide to add one or two of these to your "resiliency-builder" menu, if you think this would be useful for you.

PERSONAL RESILIENCY BUILDERS

Put a + by the top three or four resiliency builders you use most often. Ask yourself how you have used these in the past or currently use them. Think of how you can best apply these resiliency builders to current life problems, crises, or stressors. (Optional) You can then put a B (for build) by one or two resiliency builders you think you should add to your personal repertoire.

Individual Protective Factors that Facilitate Resiliency

__ Relationships – Sociability/ability to be a friend/ability to form positive relationships

__ Service/Helpfulness – Gives of self in service to others and/or a cause.

__ Life Skills – Uses life skills, including good decision-making, assertiveness, and impulse control

__ Humor – Has a good sense of humor, can laugh at difficult situations

__ Inner Direction – Bases choices/decisions on internal evaluation (internal locus of control)

__ Perceptiveness – Insightful understanding of people and situations

__ Independence – "Adaptive" distancing from unhealthy people and situations/autonomy, able to go your own way when you know it is the right way for you

__ Positive View of Personal Future – Optimism/expects a positive future

__ Flexibility – Can adjust to change; can bend as necessary to positively cope with situations

__ Love of Learning – Capacity for and connection to learning

__ Self-motivation – Internal initiative and positive motivation from within

__ Competence – Is "good at something"/personal competence

__ Self-Worth – Feelings of self-worth and self-confidence

__ Spirituality – Personal faith in something greater

__ Perseverance – Keeps on despite difficulty; doesn't give up

__ Creativity – Expressiveness through any type of artistic endeavor, and/or using imagination and creative thinking or other processes

---

Additional Excellent Resiliency-Building Resources

The following books and articles are quoted in the workbook. They are some of the best I have found; each book and article will help build your resiliency in its own unique ways. I have included them by the chapter in which I reference them in this workbook.

Quoted in Chapter One

How, Then, Shall We Live? Four Simple Questions That Reveal the Beauty and Meaning of our Lives by Wayne Muller (1996). Published by Bantam Books, New York. p. 116.

Quoted in Chapter Two

The Resilient Self: How Survivors of Troubled Families Rise Above Adversity by Steven J. Wolin and Sybil Wolin (1993). Published by Villard Books, New York. pp. 12, 15, 20.

Overcoming the Odds: High Risk Children from Birth to Adulthood by Emmy E. Werner and Ruth S. Smith (1992). Published by Cornell University Press, Ithaca, New York. p. 202.

Journeys from Childhood to Midlife: Risk, Resilience, and Recovery by Emmy E. Werner and Ruth S. Smith (2001). Published by Cornell University Press, Ithaca, New York. p. 167.

Quoted in Chapter Three

Flourish: A Visionary New Understanding of Happiness and Well-being by Martin E.P. Seligman (2011). Published by The Free Press, New York. pp. 157, 159 - 160.

Quoted in Chapter Four

"A More Humane and Effective Approach to Motivating Change" by Craig Noonan in the book *Resiliency In Action: Practical Ideas for Overcoming Risks and Building Strengths in Youth, Families, and Communities* (2007). Published by Resiliency In Action, Solvang, CA. pp. 133-136.

The Hidden Gifts of Helping: How the Power of Giving, Compassion, and Hope Can Get Us Through Hard Times by Stephen G. Post (2011). Published by Jossey-Bass, San Francisco, CA.

The Healing Power of Doing Good: The Health and Spiritual Benefits of Helping Others by Allan Luks (1991, 2001). Published by iUniverse.com, Inc., San Jose, CA.

Life Skills for Adult Children by Janet G. Woititz and Alan Garner (1990). Published by Health Communications, Inc., Deerfield Beach, FL. pp. 85 - 96.

Emotional Intelligence: Why It Can Matter More Than IQ by Daniel Goleman (1995). Published by Bantam Books, New York.

Quoted in Chapter Five

The Resilient Self: How Survivors of Troubled Families Rise Above Adversity (see chapter two above).
pp. 16 - 17.

Healing the Hardware of the Soul: Enhance Your Brain to Improve Your Work, Love, and Spiritual Life by Daniel G. Amen (2008). Published by The Free Press, New York
p. 213.

What Matters Most: Living a More Considered Life by James Hollis (2009). Published by Gotham Books, New York.
pp. 117, 40 - 41.

How, Then, Shall We Live? Four Simple Questions That Reveal the Beauty and Meaning of our Lives (see chapter one above).
p. 201.

Quoted in Chapter Six

"The Resiliency Route to Authentic Self-Esteem and Life Success" by Nan Henderson in the book *Resiliency In Action: Practical Ideas for Overcoming Risks and Building Strengths in Youth, Families, and Communities* (2007). Published by Resiliency In Action, Solvang, CA.
pp. 183 - 185.

Now, Discover Your Strengths by Marcus Buckingham and Donald O. Clifton (2001). Published by The Free Press, New York.
pp. 7 - 9, 12.

The Strengths Perspective in Social Work Practice by Dennis Saleebey, editor (1997). Published by Longman, New York.
p. 13.

Quoted in Chapter Seven

Quantum Change: When Epiphanies and Sudden Insights Transform Ordinary Lives by William R. Miller and Janet C'de Baca (2001). Published by The Guilford Press, New York.
p. 185.

Quoted in Chapter Eight

"A More Humane and Effective Approach to Motivating Change" (see chapter four above).
pp. 133-136.

Quoted in Chapter Nine

Love and Survival: 8 Pathways to Intimacy by Dean Ornish (1999). Published by Harper Collins, New York.

Glossary

These terms are in bold type throughout this workbook.

Authentic Self-Esteem
Feelings of self-worth/self-value based on one's actual strengths, competencies, accomplishments, and a connection to one's resilient core.

The Challenge Model
A resiliency-based alternative to the "Damage Model": Trauma may cause damage but according to Steve and Sybil Wolin, who developed this alternative, it is also experienced as a challenge that fosters the emergence of one's protective factors. The Challenge Model embodies each person's "capacity for self-repair," according to the Wolins.

Conscious
That aspect of the mind that includes everything inside current awareness, such as sensations, perceptions, memories, feelings, and fantasies.

The Damage Model
A traditional, "old-school" belief in psychiatry and psychology that trauma—especially in childhood—inevitably leads to lifelong psychological damage.

Emotional Intelligence
The ability to know and appropriately manage emotions, recognize and empathize with others' emotions, effectively handle personal relationships, and self-motivation.

Individuation
The process of becoming fully and uniquely oneself, a process of psychological differentiation from others and the collective whole.

Intuition
The act or faculty of knowing or sensing without the use of rational processes; an immediate "hunch" that turns out to be accurate.

Mirroring
Messages from one's environment that psychologists believe are internalized to create or impact one's self-concept.

Post-Traumatic Growth
Arriving at a higher level of psychological functioning after experiencing significant trauma, documented by research by Martin Seligman and his colleagues. Post-Traumatic Stress Disorder may precede Post-Traumatic Growth.

Post-Traumatic Stress Disorder
Re-experiencing of a traumatic event; avoiding situations that re-stimulate reactions to the traumatic event; increased emotional and/or physical arousal connected to this re-experiencing; reactions that impair social, work, or other life functioning.

Protective Factors	Internal strengths and environmental supports and opportunities that mitigate the impact of adversity and help propel people to resilient outcomes.
Resiliency	The ability to rebound, bounce-back, and transcend adversity.
The Resiliency Attitude	An attitude that embraces the concept that each person has a resilient core; the communication of the message, "What is right with you is more powerful than anything that may be wrong."
The Resiliency Wheel	A diagram developed by Nan Henderson that shows the six most powerful environmental protective factors. The Resiliency Wheel can be used by individuals, families, and organizations.
School Climate	Refers to the quality and character of school life; i.e., how students, staff, and parents experience school. It reflects norms, goals, values, interpersonal relationships, teaching and learning practices, and organizational structures.
Social and Emotional Learning	Primarily refers to K-12 training and curricula that teaches children the skills needed to handle their emotions, behaviors, relationships, and work effectively and ethically. It is a way to improve Emotional Intelligence.
Stages of Change Model	A model developed by researchers Carlo DiClemente and J.O. Prochaska describing the process by which people overcome addictions and other self-defeating behaviors. It was developed from research looking at how change occurs in "natural recovery" from addictions, and has been embraced by the move away from confrontational and pathological approaches, toward motivational and person-centered approaches.
A Strengths Perspective	A shift away from a sole emphasis on weakness and pathology to the recognition that every person—even when struggling—also has significant strengths. A Strengths Perspective emphasizes the application of these strengths to current life challenges.
Time	In relation to resiliency, "time" is the acknowledgement that a resilient outcome is a process that may happen quickly or may take many years or decades.
Unconscious	Aspects of the mind of which a person is not directly conscious or aware.

Index

Index

Order additional workbooks from
Resiliency In Action

Four ways to order

- Call toll-free 800-440-5171
- Order online at www.resiliency.com
- Fax your order to 805-691-8778
- Mail your order (with payment) to *Resiliency In Action*

> P.O. Box 1242
> Solvang, CA 93464

Discounts for quantity orders:

21 – 99 books	@ $10.95 per book
100 – 999 books	@ $9.95 per book
1,000 books or more	@ $8.95 per book

Plus 10% of total order for shipping/handling

Workshops by Nan Henderson, M.S.W.

Nan Henderson has been providing resiliency workshops across the U.S., Canada, and in other countries for the past 20 years. She speaks to educators, social service providers, parents, college students and staff, all branches of the U.S. military, and policymakers. More about her presentations, including her Resiliency Training Program Training of Trainers, is available at

www.resiliency.com

You can contact Nan Henderson directly at nhenderson@resiliency.com or at 800-440-5171.